In the Wake of Dreams

© Dave Bjorn

Cover: The wave at
'Ehukai Beach Park,
North Shore of Oahu.
'Ehukai means "sea spray".
Previous page:
Sunset, North Shore, O'ahu.
Right: Hanauma Bay, O'ahu.
Far right: Morning, Lake Waiau,
Mauna Kea, Island of Hawai'i.
Nestled in the State of Hawai'i
Ice Age Natural Area Reserve,
at 13,020' elevation, this is
the second highest U.S. lake.

Far left: Summit alpine zone cinder cone at 13,000 feet plus, Mauna Kea, Island of Hawai'i.
Left: Rain forest of 'Ohi'a trees and uluhe and 'Ama'u ferns, Volcanoes National Park, Island of Hawai'i.
Following page: Kalalau Valley, Na Pali Coast, Island of Kaua'i showing soil erosion from feral goat overpopulation.

In the Wake of Dreams

Written by
Paul Berry

Editors
Bob and Lorie Goodman

Photography
Photo Resource Hawaii

Photography Editor
Tami Dawson

Color Production
Joe Schuld

Design
Bob Goodman, David Steffen
and Mollie Yunker

The WhaleSong Collection

Dedication

To the harmony of life in Hawai'i, and
for Janet, the best sister a man ever had.

First Edition
Published by WhaleSong, Inc.
13333 Bell Red Road, Suite 230
Bellevue, WA 98005
808-595-3118 · AppleLink: WhaleSong
Copyright © 1993 WhaleSong, Inc.
Library of Congress Catalogue
Card Number 92-061390
ISBN 0-9627095-3-0
Distributed by Publishers Group West
P.O. Box 8843, Emeryville, CA 94662
1-800-788-3123.

In The Wake Of Dreams was created entirely in
PageMaker on the Macintosh color desktop with
two PixelCraft 4520 RS transparency scanners
and an Agfa Horizon flatbed scanner using
Pixelcraft QuickScan/Color Access and
Agfa FotoFlow software. All separations were
created at 200 line screen using AGFA Balanced
Screening, and output on the SelectSet 7000 imagesetter
using Agfa ZHN film and Rapid Access chemistry.
Typefaces used are Mistral, and Syntax from
The Font Company, Scottsdale, AZ.
This book was printed by Dynagraphics Printing
Co., Portland, OR. (1-800-325-8732) on
Heidelberg Speedmasters in four colors plus varnish.
Paper is Centura Dull 100 pound text, one of the world's
best printing papers from Consolidated Papers, Inc.
in Wisconsin Rapids, WI. No reproductions of words or images are
permitted, except for review purposes, without the written
consent of the publisher. For reproduction rights to the photographs
(other than for reviews) please contact Ms. Tami Dawson,
Photo Resource Hawaii, 1146 Fort Street, Suite 207,
Honolulu, Hawaii 96813, Phone: 808-599-7773.

© Franco Salmoiraghi

Postage Stamps

KINGDOM OF HAWAI'I Hawaiian 'I'iwi Honeycreeper 3¢

The idea of an island? For our people, an island is a small and precious thing, a thing that cannot be used totally. Think of it as a postage stamp, a small precious postage stamp. To live on this stamp island there are some rules. You can only live on the serrated white edge. The colored portion of the stamp belongs to *Haumea*. Belongs to *Kane*. Belongs to *Lono*. It is the place where rainwater trickles downward. This resource — our rivers are 15 miles long at the most, many of them five miles long — the idea of a river as a water resource is laughable. Our resources are very tiny, finite. The idea of extending our roads and reaching more of anything is not an idea available to us, for our roads bring us back to where we started. Our limitations as an island are not even a question of how much land we can develop, or roads we can build. The questions are more basic still, like how much water can we waste? How much do we need to drink? How much to keep the island green? This is how we, on islands, think about things. When you are the nation who today uses 32 percent of all the raw materials produced in the world yearly, you might have a hard time comprehending someone who would like to say, "It's been long past enough."

More jobs is not necessarily a song that can be sustained. It is a hope and a prayer perhaps, but not a song that can be sustained. How about more people, then? Visitors?

If you invited a million angels to an island, along with all the high qualities, positiveness and smiles they would bring — the flapping of two million wings would spread a lot of feathers around. And then you would have to ask yourself if you like feathers mixed with the leaves and other things. Even the feathers of angels can become a foreign body introduced into your area. It's not that what is introduced is wrong. It is the question, is it right for that place and that time? And the precious little thing you have, the voice within each of us, the song of the *kahu*, the keeper, the perception of the boundaries of your dream, what about that? Do you listen?

Sam Kaha'i Ka'ai
Pukalani Village, Maui

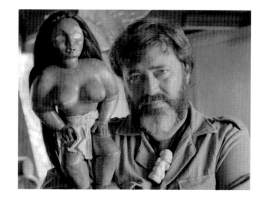

Contents

© Tami Dawson

Left: Waterfall, Waimea Falls Park,
North Shore of O'ahu.
Above: Hawaiian hula dancer.

Dreams, Dreamers and Paradise

On a group of small islands far at sea, the hand of man has been busy reshaping life. Tall trees have given way to taller buildings, ancient forests have been replaced by tree farms, and even some of the sands that visitors lie on have to be transferred from distant places. The sheer weight of human presence in Hawai'i has set off a series of major distress signals in our environment. One by one, living forms have vanished or become registrants on the Endangered Species List. Strange new flora and fauna threaten to turn the last ancient forests and birds out of the paradise they once created. Alarmed, we have moved to protect the delicate weave of island life forms by creating preserves for them, but nature is not something mankind keeps in preserves.

We have reached a turning point in the history of the islands. Adrift in a vast sea, over

Left: Outrigger canoe teams on Hanalei Bay, Kaua'i. In the background is Makana Peak, of Bali Hai fame.

a million of us live comfortable consumer lives and entertain 6.7 million visitors a year. Few of us notice that the balance between man and nature in Hawai'i is rapidly tilting. While there is cause for hope in our early steps toward conservation, as a society we appear muddled and uncertain about what we must do to save paradise. If we are to keep the web of nature which ultimately supports us, we will need a new view of man's place in nature and the courage to act on it.

Long ago I read about just such turning points in the history of societies. In Arnold Toynbee's *A Study of History,* I found a chronicle of the rise and fall of 26 civilizations. For Toynbee, the pattern of their breakup was clear. Given a serious challenge,

each had refused to change its thinking or its actions. Inevitably each collapsed.

Half a century from now, those of us deciding what happens to the life of the islands will have exited. Because they must live in the wake of our dreams, our inheritors will either thank us for our stewardship, or wonder how we could ever have been so short-sighted, so uncaring. As our choices move under the lens of history, our children will look to nature around them and tell stories of us. Somewhere in these stories, they will make it clear that we have passed along to them destruction and ugliness, or biodiversity and beauty, a dirge or a love song.

Beauty at Risk
Four Perspectives...

The Turtle

© Monte Costa

Left: Whale Shark off Lahaina, Maui.
Above: A young Green Sea Turtle, called
Honu in Hawaiian, is a threatened species,
now depleted worldwide as a result of
over-fishing, egg collecting, and tumor outbreaks.

The great green sea turtle slipped out of the shadows in the reef, late afternoon sunlight filtering across the hexagons etched across his carapace. Snorkeling along the surface a dozen feet above him, I smiled, for like me, here was a beachgoer headed out to sea. I had seen him many times before in this same passage through the reef, and as always, I turned to admire his leisurely grace, his broad shell of massive armor. As he glided toward the open sea, I stroked harder to keep up with him, for he moved like an ancient underwater bird, weightless against the current, soaring and diving without apparent effort. His head tilted slowly as he veered upward to check me out, then he resumed cruising along the reef's edge. He had seen the likes of me before, and his pace seemed to say that, although humans are predators of turtles, his armor and submarine grace were all that he needed.

My joints had felt a little creaky entering the water that day, and I wondered which of us was older. Though we were both vertebrates, the turtle was, at least in evolutionary terms, considerably older. Turtles represent the kind of evolutionary accomplishment that belongs in some kind of Darwin's Book of World Records, having survived basically unchanged for over 200 million years. Through worldwide mass extinctions of species, through ice ages, while creatures all about them changed in order to survive, turtles have clung to their original armored design. I, on the other hand, wondered why my design made it so hard to hold pace with a heavily plated creature who seemed in no real hurry. Faulty design, I concluded, for compared to the turtle, I was a still unproven evolutionary youngster. Although humans and turtles spring from the ancient era when backbones began, vertebrate human primates appeared only in the last three million years. While human evolution has benefited from some remarkable adaptations, this turtle was not only better equipped in the water, but better tested by time.

A school of a dozen ulua appeared on my right, then swept in front of me and vanished to my left. When I turned to see the turtle, I could barely distinguish its shell dissolving into the strands of flickering sunlight 15 yards ahead of me. I would have loved to tag along to see where he was going, but Hawaiian turtles migrate up to a thousand miles, and I lacked the courage to share with him the darkness melting into the open sea.

Left: An adult Honu, or Green Sea Turtle, a threatened species that is now fully protected under U.S. law. Because of this, a comeback is now in progress.
Right: Unique to Kaua'i, the Koki'o (Kokia kauaiensis), or Kaua'i Tree cotton, is a distant relative of the hibiscus.

After a slow swim back to shore, I toweled off, then sat to watch the sun float lazily into the curve of the horizon. The green sea turtle, I remembered, is a threatened species. I had enjoyed the swim, and my encounter with the beauty of the turtle had left me feeling that I had glimpsed an ancient marvel. Although he had seemed just another aging swimmer sharing the wonders of the reef, I sensed in the turtle a creature whose instincts and equipment for survival had proven more durable than those of humans. We also had a shared history, the turtle and I, creatures from a common past, now swimmers in the same place and time, in the same waters. As the light at the horizon flared and turned the clouds aglow, I was left wondering as well where our common future may lie.

Beauty and Public Business

© David Boynton

I have sometimes found myself stunned by natural beauty, moved by it as if it exercises some irresistible gravitational pull on me. I have seen it do the same to others, set them to longing for it and needing it, then leave them wordless and joyful when they have found the satisfaction that only trees or waves or moonlight can bring.

Years ago my brother and I set out before dawn for a walk in a redwood reserve on the California coast. We took our children along, and, dragged from bed earlier than usual, they were squabbling as we arrived at the head of the trail. Once in the redwoods,

18

though, with the light of dawn on the dripping ferns and the massive, soaring trunks, all conversation subsided naturally. We walked along wordless for nearly half an hour, caught up in the immensity of the force of life around us. Finally we reached the bottom of a glen where a single redwood stood separated in the morning sun. We all slowed to a stop as if on a signal. When I turned to look at my brother, he continued gazing at the wonder of the tree, then he said in a voice I could barely hear, "We would all probably do better if all public business were conducted in redwood groves."

The idea has stuck with me ever since. "We would all probably do better . . . ," all living things, from the life of the waters to the life of the land. Suppose, for example, that the Hawaii legislature were commanded to give up meeting in air conditioned buildings and

Left: Massive trunk of a dead Mehamehame tree, monarch of the dryland forests, is proposed for the endangered species list, since less than 100 survive.
Right: Koa trees (Acacia koa), dominant in Hawai'i's mid and upper forests, grow to over six feet in diameter and are prized for making Hawaiian canoes, carvings, and cabinets. Young Koa trees are often eaten and trampled by livestock.

© G. Brad Lewis

Left: The Hawaiian Short-eared Owl,
or Pueo is a sacred totem ('aumakua)
to some Hawaiian families.
Right: Rain Forest with Lobelia flower spray
(Trematolobelia), Pihea Peak, Island of Kaua'i.

© Tom Gillen

instead had to hold all of its hearings and votes, say, under a tree on the beach at Kahana Bay, or just beyond the roar of Akaka Falls on the Hamakua coast of Hawai'i , or on a windswept bluff near Seven Pools on Maui, or perhaps above the cliffs of Kaho'olawe. They would need some sunscreen, and they might get a little wet occasionally, but the legislative longing for office would see them through. They might get a little less public business done, but I firmly believe the influence of natural beauty would inevitably yield us much better laws, a much better future.

County councils, mayors, and the governor would have to follow suit as well, parking themselves in the branches of a convenient banyan tree, or convening business under the

terraced walls of, say, Moloka'i's remote Pelekunu Valley. Every vote, every signature, and every veto would occur with decision-makers having to look nature right in the eye. Public discourse would alter considerably if those setting our future course felt the pull of natural beauty, found themselves every day more a part of the people, places, and creatures they govern.

So I believe that beauty operates as a compelling influence in the lives of all humans, and the natural beauty of the Hawaiian Islands is part of what each of us unconsciously hopes to encounter every morning when we crawl out of bed. But however much or however fast we pursue this beauty, like a mirage on a desert road, it seems always to recede in front of us, to evade capture. Why, then, pursue it? Because it is only human to do so, and because the fragrance of a pikake blossom or the glimpse of a swooping pueo can fill our lives as nothing else can.

© David Boynton

23

Left: Hula halau nā Kamalei at Lanikuhonua, O'ahu.
Right: Dried seed capsules of the endangered Koki'o (Kokia drynarioides), a member of the mallow family. It is nearly extinct in the wild, where it grows on the arid lava flows of Puuwa'awa'a, North Kona.

Of Helen and Hawai'i

© G. Brad Lewis

Left: Joey Salmoiraghi, Japanese/Italian American boy.
Right: A fern fiddlehead in Wao Kele O Puna, a lowland Rain Forest, Puna, Island of Hawai'i.

In Hawai'i we rely on the beauty that surrounds us to lure visitors here. The money they spend as they enjoy the natural wonders of the islands drives the economy that supports over a million residents. With natural beauty so essential to our way of life, common sense would seem to dictate that we carefully protect our natural resources. Common sense, however, has a way of eluding us when opportunities for profit command our attention.

Consider the tale of Helen of Troy, wife of Menelaus. She was so naturally beautiful that men reportedly were sometimes afraid to look at her. When a young man of incredible beauty himself arrived as a visitor, a man by the name of Paris, she was as smitten by him as he was by her. Beauty, after all, can be irresistible. Now when Paris was born, it had been predicted that his beauty would lead to the ruin of the kingdom. Like Oedipus, he had been given to a shepherd to be disposed of, but he had survived. When Paris met Helen, he had no choice but to possess this beauty, so

© Jack Jeffrey

he carried her off across the Aegean Sea to his home in Troy on the coast of Turkey. Although she already had a child, she went willingly because Paris was simply so beautiful himself.

Prior to Helen's choice of Menelaus as her husband, the princes of the other Greek states had gathered to ask for her hand. Following good advice from Ulysses, her father made each promise to defend her chosen husband against any suitor who would resent that man's good fortune in marrying such a beauty. After she left with Paris, Menelaus in his anger called on the others to fulfill their promises to help him recapture his beautiful wife. The Greeks set out to besiege Troy, because everybody agreed that so great a loss of beauty was not to be tolerated.

Helen's face was said to be the face that launched a thousand ships. The story of the ten years of war and the power of beauty to lead to so many deaths moved Homer to create the Iliad, the first great work of litera-ture in Western civilization. It speaks of treachery, tragedy, heroism, and above all the power of beauty to motivate human beings. When Troy fell, Menelaus took Helen back with him despite her earlier betrayal of him. Why? Because she was simply so beautiful, and beauty is essential to life.

Some lessons of the story of Helen would seem to apply to the incredible natural beauty in Hawai'i .

—Whatever our cultural preconceptions, beauty will have its way with our senses, particularly what is naturally beautiful. Be-cause beauty gives us so much satisfaction and joy, we cannot ignore it.

—Whoever would own beauty, cannot, for it does not admit of ownership. The urge to control it, however, can be irresistible and usually leads to suffering. Whatever someone is willing to sacrifice in the pursuit of beauty offers others a measure of that person's sense of good and evil.

—While we perceive beauty as outside or beyond us, we know it also lies within us.

— The loss of beauty can lead to destruction, to the ruin of the kingdom. It can become the cause for treachery and tragedy, and it can also lead to acts of courage. We have within us the heroism to recapture, conserve, and defend it, if we can just find the will.

—The loss of great beauty is intolerable, for it plays an essential part in life.

Left: 'Ama'u Fern, (Sadleria), is unique to Hawai'i. The fronds were used to mulch dryland taro, and the trunk for a red dye.
Right: Hawaiian tree snail, (Pupukanioe) feeding on a leaf surface. The whole Family was listed as endangered when more than half became extinct in the 1960's to 1980's. The predators? Florida cannibal snails, rats, and human collectors.

Beauty and Survival

In nature, beauty appears to have mysterious and functional links with survival. Whether it occurs in the rain forest, atop Mauna Kea, or on the deepest ocean floors, life seems impelled to shift from sameness toward difference. The entire history of evolution is one of progressive differentiation. Humans, for example, share the same DNA, and were we to examine each of us on a subatomic level, at the level of particle and wave, we would discover ourselves to be virtually indistinguishable. Still, humans have easily discernible differences: even identical twins usually bear distinguishing marks or show marked differences in personality. We take such various forms because individually, as a species, and sometimes collaboratively, they give us a

© William P. Mull

better chance at survival. Life favors difference, and that propensity raises the question of whether difference employs beauty to enhance chances of survival.

In one of its more intriguing movements toward differentiation, life long ago tried out and found acceptable a logarithmic spiral that allowed some of its forms to create an outward, graceful curve that improved chances of survival. The form is most famous in the

chambered nautilus, a creature which came to fascinate humans. As it grows, the nautilus builds ever larger chambers to protect itself, creating a living, spiraled architecture whose form, texture, and color humans find themselves naturally drawn to. But this form appears elsewhere as well, in the swirling petals of the daisy, in the curve of the ram's horn, even in the arrangement of limbs and leaves about a tree. Apparently nature finds a purpose in what man finds beautiful.

Perhaps early humans noticed it in the distant spirals of galaxies on a clear night, or perhaps in the shell of a simple snail, but it became for them a driving force in the creations of man, from art to architecture. Somewhere in mankind's early history, a clever mind saw how the measurements of this particular outward spiral could have a parallel in the ratio of 3 to 5 (width to height) in a rectangle. This 3 to 5 ratio offered not only strength in construction, but a rectilinear shape that proved aesthetically satisfying to those who looked at it.

27

© Jack Jeffrey

for paintings, and in the buildings we create to conduct our public business.

If the shapes of physical beauty have their place in the survival of living forms, we can see and smell beauty in the attractions that flora create in order to ensure their perpetuation. Some, like the pikake and ʻilima blossoms, produce rapturously beautiful flowers and haunting scents in order to invite other forms of life to help them in pollination. Their beauty is clearly part of the mechanism that continues their species. Moreover, forms of life like bees and honeycreepers have adapted quite literally to feed on this beauty. Here beauty supplies the cause for a collaboration that supports life in all of its diversity and all of its harmony.

So beauty has a central place in the equation of life in the islands, in the very capacity that nature uses to carry growing numbers of human beings. At some point, however, the sheer weight of humanity leads to the degradation of beauty, and in the islands of

Today many of mankind's endless rectilinear shapes share the ratio found in the spiral of the chambered nautilus. We recognize it, however, only when we scrutinize rectangles to discover the ratio based on the sequence of 3 to 5, of 5 to 8, of 8 to 13, of 13 to 21, of 21 to 34, of 34 to 55, of 55 to 89, and so on. Each new number bears a rhythmically proportional balance with the number that directly precedes it. In many life forms, the spiral is approximate, but at the heart of their rhythmic, outward curling lies a ratio of .618034 to 1. It is a ratio nature has taught to man, a relationship mankind has come to call "the golden mean," and we find it in the grace of classical sculpture, in the shape of frames

Far left: A non-native Chambered Nautilus (Nautilus belauensis), breeding at the Waikiki Aquarium, was first caught off Palau in the late 1970's. The Paper Nautilus, its cousin, lives in Hawaiian waters.
Above left: The ʻIʻiwi (Vestiaria coccinea), though a common honeycreeper on the larger islands, is listed by the State of Hawaiʻi as endangered on Molokaʻi and Oʻahu.

Hawai'i, that point clearly has long since been reached. Population growth, development, feral animals, and aggressive, newly introduced species have cost the islands 50% of vital rain forests and two-thirds of their original forest cover. Today the islands have 150 natural ecological communities, 85 of them critically endangered.

The catalog of beautiful living forms and places destroyed or at risk grows longer each year. Of 93 rare plant species, 61 have only a hundred plants remaining, 21 have between two and nine individual plants, and five have only a single plant. More than half of our original bird species have vanished, and of the 70 that remain, 30 are endangered, 12 of them nearing extinction. Hanauma Bay on Oahu, long a symbol of the striking beauty of Hawai'i's waters, has become a leading visitor attraction. Inundated now by thousands of visitors and residents who want to enjoy its waters, the bay has suffered substantial damage to its reefs, water quality, and ecological balance.

Across the islands, distress signals from nature continue to arrive with increasing frequency, almost as if beauty were crying out for rescue.

The natural impulse of island life to survive, adapt, and differentiate seems to be reversing, collapsing under the growing human presence. Contrary to what the book of *Genesis* tells us, nature does not exist to serve mankind, for beyond serving us, it must serve a rich mixture

of other life forms as well. Mankind has carved out a place in nature, and if we require too large a place and destroy nature's balance, we must eventually face the same consequences as the species we push to-

© David Boynton

ward extinction. Among all of Earth's life forms, only mankind can grasp the mysterious and functional place of diversity and beauty in the ecosystem. But if we cannot find the will to conserve and defend what supports us, human understanding will have meant nothing.

Above: A descendant of pigs brought by early Polynesian voyagers, then crossed with European stock. The feral pig is too abundant in some Hawaiian forests, where it feeds by rooting up the topsoil, exposing and breaking the shallow roots of native plants. Right: The upper Kamakou Preserve is a Cloud Forest on Moloka'i. Managed by The Nature Conservancy, it is one of Hawai'i's most pristine habitats.

30

Distant Arrivals

© Jack Jeffrey

Above: 'Ohi'a lehua blossom on lichen covered 'a'a lava near the Saddle Road, Island of Hawai'i.
Right: The beloved Kumu Hula, Edith Kanakaole and her daughters, Pua and Nalani, at the rim of Kilauea Caldera, the Island of Hawai'i.

Millions of years before the arrival of man, life began to emerge in the Hawaiian islands. Scientists tell us that the seamounts of the northern islands in the archipelago began to form some 70 million years ago. As the northern islands were subsiding, the islands we populate began to rise, Oahu four million years back, and the island of Kaua'i just over five and a half million years ago. Contemporary man evolved roughly within the last three million years, but the best estimates suggest that only in the last 1,800 years has there been a human presence in Hawai'i. Up to that point these islands remained like Eden before Adam, akin to the earth that *Genesis* describes for us during the first five days of creation.

Afloat in a distant sea, over 2,400 miles from the nearest land mass, these beautifully dowered islands created an interweaving of life uniquely their own, one which evidently flourished without man. In finding this paradise, the Hawaiians reached out to discover one of earth's last untouched possibilities.

If humans have arrived only in the last few ticks of earth's clock, we have competed with impressive success, establishing an evolutionary foothold, then moving to control the rich

34

Above right: The Hawaiian hoary bat,
'ope'ape'a in Hawaiian, an endangered species,
is the Islands' only native land mammal. An insect eater,
this bat sleeps in trees and comes out to feed at dusk.
Above: The Hawaiian Happyface Spider spins a
tiny web under leaves and uses its long legs
to lasso passing prey with silk. This male's
marks are a mystery to scientists.
Right: The Ambushing Inchworm is Hawai'i's extra-
ordinary answer to the Praying Mantis
found on the continents. It is the world's only
rapacious predator among caterpillers.

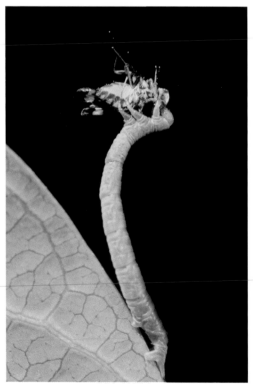

Opposite page: An Anchialine pool,
with freshwater floating on denser salt-
water, is home to 'Opae'ula and many
other unique shrimp. One species was
named after the late Governor John Burns,
who had protected its home on Maui as a
State Natural Area Reserve on Cape Kinau
at Ahihi Bay. Connected to the ocean
by underground fissures, many of these
unique habitats on the Big Island were
bulldozed to build the Waikoloa Resort.

array of life forms that long preceded us. Any new species inevitably makes its mark on the neighborhood, and, with the arrival of humankind, the islands were forever altered.

Until humans ventured here, life in Hawai'i had accommodated only the ongoing volcanic creation of the islands, and the random arrival of new life forms. From perhaps a thousand original species, native terrestrial biota of the Hawaiian chain have evolved into most of the estimated 10,000 to 15,000 species we now have here. While we have some records of unusual early creatures, we have yet to determine how many species expired prior to the arrival of man. First evidence suggests they are few. Recent hurricanes and the volcanic extravaganzas on the island of Hawai'i remind us that the angry earth can extinguish some of the forms it gives life to. With 6,425 square miles of land surrounded by 70 million square miles of ocean, the ebb and flow of life in Hawai'i creates the most unusual evolutionary laboratory in the world.

This small world of its own originally had no amphibians, no reptiles, few freshwater fishes, and only a pair of mammals, the monk seal and the hoary bat. Distance meant exclusivity for smaller creatures as well, for Hawai'i had only about a half of the world's Orders of insects. Hawaiian land and tree snails once abounded, appearing in 800 species, some attaching themselves to only a few kinds of trees. Neither Darwin nor his evolutionary counterpart Wallace ever ventured to the islands, but Darwin was quoted as saying, "I would give 50 pounds to any man who would collect for me at the Sandwich Islands."

In evolutionary terms, the definition of the word "original" is curious to contemplate, for unlike today, over the millions of years of evolution before man, it was a long time between immigrants. Naturalists speculate that original species established themselves here about once every 70,000 years. For

birds, 15 original ancestors, or about one new species every 5,000,000 years, eventually evolved into 70 species. "Original" speaks of origins, life at its creation, but because we now know that local creatures such as the golden plover are given to extraordinary feats

© Monte Costa

Left: Nectar rich flower of the Hau Kuahiwi (Hibiscadelphus hualalaiensis) an old Hawaiian genus unique to this archipelago. This tree, now dead, was the last remaining in the wild. Seeds have been propagated, and once cattle and goats are controlled, this tree can be reintroduced.
Above: Monk Seal photographed at Sea Life Park. Their program helps protect the injured females, as there are fewer than 1,500 Monk Seals remaining.

of migration (i.e., they might be considered to have origins elsewhere), for practical reasons the term "original" might best be defined as *established prior to the arrival of man.*

The earth, the giver of life, reminds us of the origins of islands, making regular yet spectacular deliveries of its hot inner secrets on the island of Hawai'i. It also acts as a destroyer via cataclysm (volcanism, hurricane, tsunami) as well as a sculptor via heat, cold, water, and wind weathering. The volcanic coast of Hawai'i appears forged in the fires of *Pele,* the Hawaiian goddess of fire. Here vast sweeps of molten lava have piled layer upon layer to form a crusted carpet of stony black. Belched upward from superheated depths to create new land, the landscape of black would seem to defy the attempt of any life forms to find survival on it. Flowing lava turns trees suddenly to fire, and sets luckless houses to flame. Then, as it rolls into the pounding surf, it creates a deep-throated rush of sound and dancing clouds of steam, the sigh and breath of earth, then the fiery kiss of earth and sea.

38

The Big Island has seen repeated rivers of lava destroy organisms which had arrived to eke out an existence on it after a previous eruption. To walk such a harsh, blackened landscape is to feel yourself only one small place-holder in the equation balancing life at the earth's surface. Whatever our evolutionary adaptations, each living form must face the raw force of the earth, and each of us must scramble to find a perch to survive what roars up from below. During the most recent eruption of Mauna Loa, for example, I arrived at the 11,000 foot level to watch wordlessly the roaring 150 foot fountain of lava as it built into a stream of molten fire that pooled and splashed. Finding a break in the ridge, it built into a river that plummeted down the mountainside. Against a dull sky crowded with sulphurous clouds, the angry orange fountain made it clear that man did not belong here. I could not help wondering if the steady roar of spewing lava was but a whisper before the earth found its full voice. Here the power of nature spoke clearly, humbling all life before it.

Many early forms of life on the islands vanished not from cataclysm, but through the give and take of evolutionary struggle, a struggle altered dramatically by the arrival of humans. They emerge as distant echoes sounded from contemporary paleontological

© G. Brad Lewis

Opposite page: Kilauea Volcano on the Island of Hawai'i has been continuously active for the past eight years. It continues to add new land mass to the island chain as it pours into the sea. Left: Waterspouts are small tornadoes over the ocean, lasting but a few moments and only occasionally coming ashore.

© G. Brad Lewis

40

and archeological digs. We have learned quite recently, for example, that the island of Hawai'i had a huge, flightless goose weighing five times as much as the contemporary nene, i.e., some 20 to 25 pounds. At that size, it would have been the largest land creature on the islands prior to man. The bird could climb, for its remains were found some 4,600 feet up Hualalai, above the Kona coast. Such a creature, zoologists tell us, is like the Moa of New Zealand, an evolutionary island equivalent of a plant eating dinosaur or a large mammal found on the continental land masses, or the giant tortoise of the Galapagos Islands.

Large flightless birds also suggest an absence of mammalian and ground living predators, so from the great bird's presence we can infer something about the species that did not find their way here before man. Scientists believe that without terrestrial predators, birds may evolve toward having no capacity for flight. How the bird got here and evolved into its lumbering ancient self is only part of a larger story of many creatures, including some 20 other flightless birds that vanished into extinction, mostly as a result of early Polynesian presence.

As they have for millennia, creatures continue to find their ways here. In the late 1960's scientists reported finding a lone golden eagle in the uplands of Kaua'i. A difficult animal to smuggle in, the soaring creature must have been surprised by a storm and blown here from the North America or Siberia. The eagle's arrival lent support to the surmises of scientists that life forms have from the beginning arrived in the islands seaborne or windborne, surviving trips that boggle the imagination. A generation ago, for example, two poisonous sea snakes common to the South Pacific were reported dead on the windward side of Oahu. Current riders? Long distance swimmers? They left no clues as to their means of transportation.

In the hope of capturing life on its way toward the islands, several scientists have suspended nets from airplanes and the masts of ships. Among the life forms they have caught between sea level and four thousand feet were windborne spiders and plant lice. Whatever our pride in man's command of the skies, nature over the millennia has fashioned its own forms of transportation.

Anticipating future needs, the first human visitors here carried with them a variety of living things that had served them well on other islands. The canoe became a miniature ark of creatures calculated to ensure human survival: pig, jungle fowl, dog, and 26 plants, including coconut, kukui, breadfruit, sugarcane, yams, wauke, taro, ti, bamboo, and

© Marc Schechter

Opposite page: Kilauea's most recent vent, Episode 51, pouring a river of lava toward the sea.
Above: The Nene, the only surviving Hawaiian goose, is still endangered by predators, though many goslings have been propagated and released on Maui and Hawai'i by the State. Another group escaped from captivity and is re-establishing itself on Kaua'i due to a lack of the Indian mongoose.

42

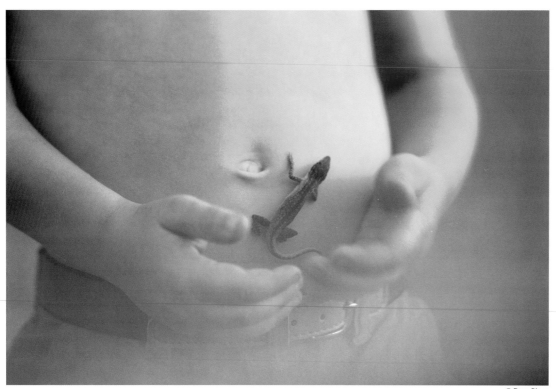

© Dave Bjorn

indigo. Several other travelers, probably inadvertent, were the flea, the louse, four geckos, three skinks, and the rat. The impact of humans and their living cargo was probably slow at first, for it took time for the arrivals to build populations and move among the islands. Still, the arrival of so many species in the company of man marked a point of no return in the life of the islands. For the first time conscious minds were now moving to control the score of the great random symphony of life.

Traditional Hawaiian culture had at its center a consciousness of natural life that speaks of the best of human qualities — humility and wisdom. Archeological evidence indicates, however, that this regard for nature apparently required some time to evolve. Early humans took a toll on some parts of the environment, for flightless birds were hunted to extinction, moist and dry forests were

© G. Brad Lewis

cleared by fire, and pigs were occasionally allowed to run feral. But with no possibility of help from the outside, Hawaiians developed a consciousness of the need to conserve nature, a sense of oneness with other living forms. From the creation myth found in the *Kumulipo,* to their spiritual beliefs, to their most ordinary daily acts, they had created by the time of Cook's arrival an environmentally conscious economy that balanced agriculture

with hunting and fishing. As the remnants of over 60 fishponds on the leeward side of Moloka'i tell us, they were also adept with aquaculture, something high tech modern man still struggles to master. Division of land into ahupua'a left each group in control of a wedge of territory ranging from highlands to offshore waters. This arrangement meant the handling of taro patches and wastes from animals held consequences for shoreline fishing.

With no possibility of help from the outside, hope for an abundant life kept Hawaiians conscious of the need to conserve nature. The Hawaiian population flourished and peaked, probably in the mid 17th century. While their total numbers at the point of Cook's arrival in 1778 remain a matter of speculation, it seems clear that Hawaiian wisdom included a sense of a sustainable human population in the face of limited natural resources.

The addition of man also foreshadowed the later impact of human technology as an evolutionary force in the history of the islands. Human arrival across the Pacific had to wait for early Polynesians to accomplish technologically and intellectually what no one else had yet accomplished (and all but a few living people still cannot accomplish);

44

they had to create vessels and master navigation that would allow voyagers to survive a venture thousands of miles into an unknown sea. Accustomed to seeing the Pacific as their continent and its islands as their cities, these bold explorers gave wings to their dreams. We have no way of knowing of the losses they suffered in attempting these extraordinary voyages, what tolls the sea and the weather took of the bravest and the best of navigators. But with human beings came human technology, the precursors of the chainsaw, the smokestack, and the cement truck.

As artist Herb Kane suggests superbly in his painting *The Discovery of Hawai'i,* what the voyagers found here after so long a journey must have stunned them. Kane depicts them

© G. Brad Lewis

at dusk, caught in the glow of fiery explosions and lava flows from the nearing volcanic shore. They are relieved to find land, yet awed by Pele's extravagant greeting. How life forms here have responded to the human presence is an ongoing story that has recently taken a dark turn, for the understandings humans reached with nature long ago now appear lost in our dreams of growth.

Like these original visitors, each of us now on the shores of paradise will leave a mark on nature, and with it a legacy for those who follow. On what Mark Twain called "the loveliest fleet of islands that lies anchored in any ocean," mankind's willingness to strike new working agreements with nature has become the central question of our time.

Opposite page: Taro patch at sunset in Hanalei National Wildlife Refuge, a wetland set aside to protect Hawai'i's four endangered waterbirds (the duck, coot, stilt, and moorhen).
Left: Ancient chants echo across Wao Kele O Puna after the rain forest was bulldozed for geothermal development.

Moloka'i Water Blues

© Franco Salmoiraghi

To the casual eye, the island of Moloka'i looks like a place where nothing seems to change much. The mountains of the east end rise steeply to meet moist clouds, the west end spreads like a scarred veldt toward Oahu, and below the northern cliffs, the tiny peninsula of Kalaupapa huddles against the steady wind coming off the north Pacific, its memories of Father Damien fading.

In its own way, however, Moloka'i has come to symbolize the struggles between destruction and conservation that mark the eight major Hawaiian islands. Here 6,500 or so residents, mostly Hawaiians, hold a fierce love for their island, for it has a sleepy magic and beauty found nowhere else in the archi-

pelago. Although they need jobs, they have come to view any suggested change with a caution approaching suspicion. Over the years, people from the outside have seen in Moloka'i's dreamy pace and open spaces opportunities for their own grand economic designs. While the island has become a graveyard for such enterprises, inevitably some of them have left the residents of Moloka'i to live with the debris that floats in the wake of broken dreams.

When you look at a landscape in an unpopulated area, it is easy to assume that what you see represents natural history. As you travel up toward the cliffs overlooking Kalaupapa, however, what you see is a chronology of changes brought by humans, changes mirrored today in many places in Hawai'i. As they have throughout the world, grazing animals came and began reshaping the ecosystems of Moloka'i. In the 1790's Captain George Vancouver set cattle loose to graze on the island of Hawai'i, and a little over a decade later, they were brought to Moloka'i and left to graze most of the island.

In the second half of the 19th century, Axis deer arrived as a gift of the king of Siam. In much the same fashion that they have throughout the island chain, the cattle, goats and deer left native foliage and grasses depleted, their damage compounded by feral pigs roaming the forests. In the cool, native forests on the heights of Pala'au, these animals eventually reduced the ohia, koa, and other resident species so badly that the forest lost its environmental balance and all but died out.

What then followed demonstrates the hazards of allowing man to take charge of the environment. In place of native plants, newcomers introduced ironwood, Norfolk pine, eucalyptus, and Australian paperbark trees.

© Alan Goya

Opposite page: Mo'omomi Dunes, the best preserved coastal habitat, now managed by The Nature Conservancy.
Above: Plantation of Australian Ironwood trees (Casuarina). A monoculture forest like this displaces Hawaiian wildlife. Decomposing ironwood foliage prevents any competing growth.

Right: Typical valley bottom Polynesian rain forest at Wailau, Moloka'i. Kukui trees (Candlenut), 'Ohi'a 'Ai (Mountain Apple), and a carpet of 'Awapuhi (Shampoo Ginger) edges the stream bed. The sign saying "Malama" means to care for and preserve. Opposite page: The elfin plants of Pepe'opae Bog, Moloka'i: 'Ohia Lehua, 'Uki Sedge, Pukiawe, Hoi Kuahiwi (Briarless Greenbriar), are all protected because this area is under active management by The Nature Conservancy.

© Tami Dawson

Those in charge of the planting did not understand that by covering a wide area with a single new species, then an adjoining area with another, they might deny native species a place to survive. In the groves of ironwood and eucalyptus today, you will find only a spare scattering of other species on the floor, for man cannot match nature in creating the rich diversity of natural forests.

No one dreamed that the new trees might even begin to alter the weather on the heights, but some longtime residents of the heights are convinced it is true. Older residents remember the rain in this area as great fat drops that splattered when they landed, the product of much heavier, taller clouds that used to cling to what some called the cloud forest. Hawaiians remember these rain drops as well, for they were said to bake when they fell on the he'eiau Na'imu Ka'lua Ua (the oven that bakes the raindrops) of the sacred highlands of Na'iwa, above Kualapu'u and Ho'olehua.

Though they can stay wet for weeks, the heights of Pala'au, Na'iwa and Kala'e no longer have rain drops that splatter and bake. More, the water these heights once supplied to the aquifers for Ho'olehua's farms has dwindled. With the best of intentions, newcomers set off a chain of consequences no one predicted. If you walk this man-made

forest today, you may see at its edges a few koa trees still clinging to the land, their valuable hardwood untouched. But walking through the ironwoods, then the eucalyptus, you will see only ironwoods, then only eucalyptus. Ironwoods cover the forest floor with heavy needles, leaving little chance for anything else to find a purchase on the soil. The man-made forest has also begun to make inroads on the rich mixture of mountain plants in the primeval forest adjoining it to the east.

Into this unfolding story of clouds, trees, and water have stepped enterprising people from off island and the farmers from Hawaiian Homestead lands. A controversial golf course-resort planned for the highlands of nearby Na'iwa, and a major development planned for the distant west end raise new concerns about water for the Hawaiian Homestead farmers in dry Ho'olehua. Anticipated increases in demand have created a need for more precise scientific measurements of just how much water anyone can expect to draw from the watershed. Estimates range from demand for three or four times the present use to 100 times more. In the fall of 1992 water researchers embarked on a two year study to define the minimum flows

© Franco Salmoiraghi

Above: Moloka'i resident and child, Kaunakakai.
Right: View of north coast valleys and 'Okala Islet from Kalawao, Kalaupapa, Moloka'i.

needed to support first the rain forest watershed, then any demands from farming or enterprise beyond.

As it has elsewhere in the islands, The Nature Conservancy wisely anticipated this situation. The non-profit organization had acquired the Kamakou preserve incorporating rain forest and bogs in the highlands, and Pelekunu Valley, the very areas new enterprises have come to covet for their additional water. Pelekunu sends more than 50 million gallons of water a day rushing into the sea and supports unique Hawaiian stream life. Meanwhile, those who would further develop the west end talk of building a 24" water pipeline, hoping to avoid the water blues, though they as yet have no water permit. And developers who scraped a broad road in the red dirt up into the highlands toward Na'iwa continue to seek a permit for water to build a golf course and residential development.

On small islands the scarcity of water forces people to make choices that reveal what they value most. In precontact times the leeward shore of Moloka'i held some 60

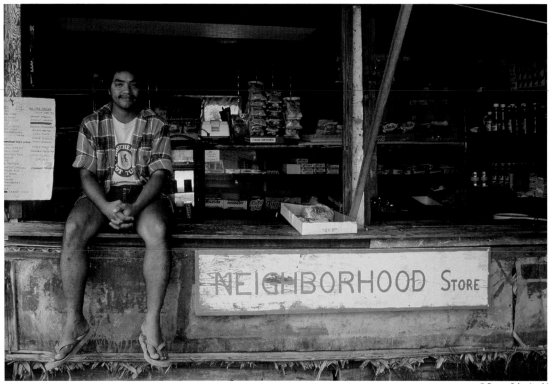

© Franco Salmoiraghi

fishponds, testimony to the skills of Hawaiians for generating aquaculture. Streams once descended the leeward face of the central mountains to feed these ponds, but many of the streams no longer regularly flow. The fishponds are mostly gone now, their bottoms silted in, some overgrown with grasses and introduced mangroves. Moloka'i's fishponds represent man in the past arriving at an agreeable compromise with nature. They represent as well what happens when man loses touch with nature and stops caring for forest watershed, a loss of direction that ignores the future.

An incomplete chronicle of change on Moloka'i includes tales of brave starts and unexpected endings. Environmental damage seems to arrive as a common outcome of economic dreams. In the 1920's this island was briefly the bee capital of the world, sending honeybees off to beekeepers in distant places. Then a disease devastated the bee industry, ending that adventure and leaving Moloka'i short of bees. With the advent of pineapple came the need to redistribute water to make plants flourish from the rolling slopes of Kualapu'u to Maunaloa to the shores of Mo'omomi. Eventually a man-made, rubber-lined reservoir was built in Kualapu'u, but then competition from abroad doomed pineapple, which dwindled and eventually vanished in the 1980's. Through pineapple days and thereafter, dusty topsoil swept down to the leeward shallows, leaving a rusty scar reaching toward the distant reef.

Twice since mid-century all the cattle on Moloka'i have been slaughtered as a result of outbreaks of bovine tuberculosis. Cattle again roam the denuded sweep of the west end, and erosion cuts red gashes that feed occasional runoff toward the leeward shallows and the sands of Mo'omomi. An innovative power plant designed to use biomass was installed, but when it failed, it left fewer trees standing, a power plant still burning oil, and Moloka'i islanders with the highest cost of electricity in America. A small curl of smoke now drifts inland on still days, and the CO_2 rises silently to the skies. A planned residential development on the heights east of Kaunakakai failed, the lots auctioned off. Grasses again cover the hillsides, but the fish ponds below still carry the silt from that development.

In the summer of 1991, a fire swept much of the mountain side behind Kaunakakai, miraculously sparing houses, but devastating the grasses and scattered plant life of the lower leeward slopes. At night the fire moved like the hand of Pele, but it had a human origin. The grasses, however, returned rapidly once the rains came. In the main town of Kaunakakai, outside Friendly Market, and down by Moloka'i Wines and Spirits, and in Kanemitsu's Bakery, quiet conversations turn toward questions of development, toward fruit flies troubling the melon growers, and toward what will happen to the island's water.

Off the beaten path of tourism, Moloka'i has seen change come and go, but on the leeward lowlands, on the windswept west end, and along the heights above Kala'e, the environment reveals a tapestry of changes brought by man. Moloka'i's scarcity of water and depressed economy would seem to make it an unlikely candidate for rapid growth, but new enterprise sits waiting to see how much it can borrow from nature. In the early 1990's, a visitor might see in this Hawaiian island a microcosm of the larger struggle to preserve the environment throughout the islands.

Along the cloud covered rainforests and ridges, however, the ancient plants and delicate creatures conduct life as they have for millennia. And below the people wonder if Moloka'i has now become an environmental laboratory, a focal point for contending economic, political, and conservation forces, a place for new seekers of water and the controversy water brings to the land.

© David Boynton

As the catalogue shows, to err is human, and residents sometimes get unexpected opportunities to feel what the rest of living things suffer via military training. Recently artillery shells from the Schofield Range have whistled all the way over the Waianae mountains and landed on the high slopes above the Waianae coast. Residents below were left more than a little uneasy. On one occasion, a misguided pilot dropped a bomb on Ni'ihau but fortunately missed everyone. Another dropped a bomb near a vessel that had strayed into a Navy firing range. And during Maui's years of rapid development, one errant pilot missed Kaho'olawe by 15 miles and dropped a 500 pound bomb on Maui land ranched by the mayor. There is no record of anyone there claiming the incident was a comment on rapid growth.

Left below: World War II shell rusting in the Ka'u Desert, Island of Hawai'i.
Right: Morning view of Maui's Haleakala shield volcano from Kaho'olawe Island's Hakioawa Bay. The Ohana that protects this island comes ashore here.

The War With Nature

© Pat Duefrene

Although dedicated to carrying out public policy in defending our lands, the U.S. Defense Department over the last 50 years has created a Jekyl and Hyde record in its treatment of the environment. At times the military has acted as a model citizen, going to extraordinary lengths to protect endangered species. More often, however, it has treated the land and the water with a savage recklessness, leaving environmental damage that may last for many generations. Looking at the unfolding record, across the country and particularly in Hawai'i, it would be easy to conclude that the real loser of the Cold War has been nature.

Individual cases of environmental destruction on a national scale reveal a frightening pattern in our defense establishment. In southeastern Indiana, for example, the U.S.

Army has spent 50 years testing conventional weapons at the Jefferson Proving Grounds. Parts of the site are contaminated with unexploded ordnance, toxic sludge, and low level radioactive wastes. Although they have the responsibility for cleaning up this environmental damage, the Army now says cleanup of Jefferson is impossible because of the cost ($13 billion) and the impact bulldozing would cause. They intend to close its 100 square miles of land and, rather amazingly, expect to fence it off from human use — forever.

Left: U.S. Army convoy from PTA (Pohakuloa Training Area) on the Saddle Road at Waiki'i on Parker Ranch.
Right: Kaho'olawe gully showing military attempt at erosion control. On October 22nd, 1990, President Bush directed the Secretary of Defense to immediately discontinue use of Kaho'olawe as a weapons firing range while Congress studies methods to return it to civilian control.

The pattern of environmental callousness holds true for defense contractors as well. In the central valley of California, for example, it was recently revealed that Aerojet General, a huge military contractor, for 23 years polluted 8,400 acres of land and eight trillion gallons of ground water with 161 chemicals and toxins from its rocket factories. Deadly chemicals such as trichloroethylene found their way from unlined settling ponds into nearby drinking water wells and the American River, which residents use heavily for recreation. Called to task when the damage was uncovered, the contractor billed the Defense Department to cover the cleanup as a "cost of doing business." The Pentagon has so far given $38

© Tami Dawson

million to Aerojet to cover the cost of a cleanup that could run a bill of $150 million.

Across the country in community after community, authorities have uncovered massive toxic damage caused by the ten largest defense contractors. The pending cost to American taxpayers is estimated at $5 billion, and no one speaks of the poisoned life forms. The list of polluters includes some famous names in American business, among them General Electric, Lockheed, General Motors, General Dynamics, and Martin Marietta Corporation.

These tragedies have their analogs in Hawaiʻi's experience with the military services, where several unfortunate cases magnify the hazards of having a significant military presence operating on so small a land area. Although federal laws protect the environment, and funds remain available for cleaning it up and restoring it, federal defense agencies in Hawaiʻi have frequently ignored their responsibilities to restore the land. Instead they often seem more interested in blunting attempts to require them to act responsibly.

Military descriptions of environmental damage raise echoes of the Newspeak issued by George Orwell's Ministry of Truth in his novel 1984. Consider a few of the phrases and acronyms these federal agencies have added to the curious lexicon of environmental trouble: ordnance/explosive waste — OEW; formerly used defense sites — FUDS; Defense Environmental Restoration Program — DERP. Translate OEW as unexploded bombs and ammunition, some of them buried just under topsoil, and read FUDS as abandoned bases with devastated forests, and badly chewed up terrain that may include OEW. DERP looks like a fund aimed at repairing military environmental damage, but for want of coordination or interest in owning up to damage done, the funds often are not spent.

While waste that can explode is relatively new to human history, it is even newer in the islands. The bombing of Pearl Harbor marked the only significant military hostilities of this century in Hawaiʻi. Preparation for World War II, however, and a half century of cold war have left a tragic legacy of devastation here.

© Jon K. Ogata

The public has heard often about bomb damage to Kahoʻolawe and the mortar fire buried in Makua Valley on Oahu, but the environmental damage by the military in Hawaiʻi extends beyond what many of us have ever imagined. In her thoughtful and thorough publication *Environment Hawaiʻi*, Patricia Tummons reviews a 1990 Defense Department report listing 230 contaminated sites in Hawaiʻi, only one of which had been cleaned up as of

Right: U.S. Navy dump on Kahoʻolawe Island. In March of 1993 the Kahoʻolawe Island Conveyance Commission issued their extensive recommendations for clean-up of the island to the U.S. Congress.

© G. Brad Lewis

the date of the report. Pearl Harbor alone has some 40 contaminated sites, some threatening to leach toxins into the water table. With funds for cleanup available since 1984, it seems reasonable to ask why the Army Corps of Engineers and the military agencies involved have not acted.

A closer look suggests that the military sometimes acts as if the land under its control will never, perhaps cannot ever, have another use. In Hawaiʻi U.S. military services have refused to comply with laws governing the environment, and have ignored agreements with property owners. From a military point of view, annual Congressional hearings review their cleanup of military waste sites, but Congress has no teeth. Confronting any branch of the American military, even the EPA is power-

less to enforce the law, for a Reagan era directive still in effect requires Justice Department approval for any one branch of the government to sue another branch. Such approval rarely arrives.

Citing the case of the Kamaka family lands in Waikane Valley in her newsletter, Tummons chronicles the callousness of those in charge of cleaning up OEW and FUDS.

According to Tummons, although the Army Corps of Engineers has a "dollar rich" program available to clean up defense sites, a memo from a Bush era commander (Pacific Division, Naval Facilities Engineering Command) refuses to authorize funds from the Defense Environmental Restoration Account (DERP) to clean up explosives embedded in Waikane Valley. A lease with the Kamakas granted the military use of the land for bombing and shelling, but in it the military promised to clear the land and to return it in the condition in which they originally found it. Military use of the land ended in the early 1960's, but the damage has left the Kamakas unable to use their hillsides thereafter.

Given the notice to vacate, the Marines did so in the mid-1970's, but since then they have refused to make good on their promise to clean up OEW. After hauling away over 28 tons of unexploded ordnance and examining the land several times, the Marines declared the site beyond cleanup. An independent civilian report held otherwise, setting a cleanup price above $7 million. The Kamakas have insisted on holding the government to the agreement to deliver the land free of explosives; the land has lo'i (for taro growing) and a number of archeological sites of spiritual significance to Hawaiian culture. In response, the government has undertaken condemnation of the land and hopes to fence it off forever from further use. The Kamakas figure "forever" is a little longer than they had hoped to wait. At press time, a federal court verdict had just been issued against them.

Considering that the federal government owns over 10% of the land mass of Hawai'i, and leases thousands of acres more for military uses, any reasonable person would have to look at the plight of the Kamakas and question if the federal government will continue to refuse accountability for its treatment of fragile island land. If the Defense Department can flagrantly neglect laws and legal agreements, then successfully condemn land and buy its way out of its responsibilities, should we reasonably expect the military to conserve and protect island lands? Or should we expect them to condemn training areas piece by piece and fence them in? In this scenario, we have to wonder how much the Defense Department will leave us that will be worth defending.

The long and tragic misuse of Kaho'olawe as a shelling range by American and allied armed forces provides a different example of the military resisting any limitations. Publicity surrounding the lawsuit over the shelling of the island, the rise of Hawaiian activism, and political pressure from the Protect Kaho'olawe 'Ohana finally led to a legal agreement limiting military uses of the island. Although the Navy has yet to give up further use of the island, by the summer of 1992, it had cleared enough of the land to allow students to visit

the Hawaiian cultural sites. And in late August of 1992, the Protect Kaho'olawe 'Ohana and the Office of Hawaiian Affairs were celebrating partial restoration of the island. Dressed in a kihei, Governor John Waihe'e listened as his genealogy was chanted at the dedication of a temple to Hawaiian ancestors.

Recently the Department of Defense has begun to fulfill some of its responsibilities under the Endangered Species Act and the Environmental Protection Act. The military has approved four cooperative projects with the Nature Conservancy of Hawai'i to begin environmental surveys of the flora and fauna on 14,000 acres of the Schofield Barracks Military Reservation, including parts of both the Ko'olau and Waianae mountain ranges. According to The Nature Conservancy, these areas are among the more biologically diverse in the entire state, containing 45 of Hawai'i's rarest plant and animal species. Scientists will do similar surveys on the upper reaches of the heavily bombarded Makua Valley, the Kawailoa Training Area in the remote central highlands of the Ko'olaus, and in the Kanaio Training Area on the southern slopes of Haleakala on Maui. The four projects are funded with $655,000 from the Defense Department's Legacy Resource Management Program, which hopes to establish comprehensive information on the biological and archeological status of lands long under military control. While the Legacy effort constitutes a good, if belated, beginning, most of the 250,000 acres of island land under Department of Defense control have never had any kind of ecological survey.

The Navy's Pearl Harbor National Wildlife Refuge goes a step farther, offering a model of environmental responsibility. Concerned about loss of habitat for birds displaced when the state built the reef runway at Honolulu Airport, the Navy has, since the late 1970's, collaborated with the U.S. Fish and Wildlife Service to construct and maintain two sizable habitats for endangered Hawaiian ducks, stilts, coots, and moorhens. In what seems like a case of environmental schizophrenia, this bird-loving Naval agency turns out to be the same one that refuses to clean up the Kamaka's devastated lands in Waikane Valley. Just when Dr. Jekyl has charmed us, the dark nature of Mr. Hyde appears.

If Kahoʻolawe and the Pearl Harbor Wildlife Refuge offer hope, the fences across Makua Valley and the Kamaka lands of Waikane Valley speak of continuing danger, controversy, and need for action. Damage in areas out of the public eye and entirely under military control remains the stuff of veiled and flawed federal reports. Without full public disclosure of the condition of these lands, we have no way to hold accountable those given a public trust. Essential questions remain unanswered. What of the ration containers and ammunition boxes scattered across the mountain side at Pohakuloa on the island of Hawaiʻi? What will scientists find at the Schofield Range in the Waianaes and at the Kawailoa training area? What is yet to be discovered at the Wahiawa training center and blast range in the central Koʻolaus? And

© Jack Jeffrey

Left: Hawaiian Stilt (Ae'o) in Taro patch.

what of the Navy weapons testing laboratory in Lualualei Valley? What of the hazards of atomic weapons stored on Oahu for use on American nuclear submarines?

As we sit at the brink of a new era in the role of our national defenses, opportunities to reclaim significant parts of Hawai'i's environment appear on the rise. Of the 3,500 military sites around the country that have unexploded ordnance, explosive wastes, or serious toxic contamination, some 7% are in Hawai'i. With federal budget deficits soaring, the military faces funding cuts that may lead it to relinquish some bases and cut back on others. But just as it does in war, the military in peace does not yield anything easily.

Shrinking military budgets may also mean less funding available for repairing and restoring nature at damaged and poisoned bases. Nonetheless, as forces shrink, our opportunities for restoration will come, and to paraphrase Barry Goldwater, opportunism in defense of nature is no vice.

As the record reveals, the military often seems careless, inclined to do environmentally whatever is easiest for those making the decisions. Destruction comes easily to those called on to use nature for target practice. Conservation, however, takes work and care and patience, and those are tough qualities to expect from people who are paid little and moved to another base every two or three years. Still, the irony is glaring. These forces are primarily charged with protecting our lands. To believe we must choose between nature and the careless practice of defense is to suffer a tragic failure of the imagination.

While nationally the Defense Department commits millions of taxpayer dollars to pay for the pollution created by its weapons systems contractors, the military has yet to establish practices to prevent environmental damage and reduce pollution. Although it has $3.7 billion in DERP, it spends only half of the money in cleaning up government-owned sites. As we have seen locally, it also feels no urgent need to clean up what it has devastated. So while hopes for salvaging Hawai'i's military sites are on the rise, they are tethered by politics and the lack of leadership. If the natural environment of Hawai'i is to recover from the long cold war, those who control the military must undergo at the deepest levels a change of heart and a change of values.

Scarcity teaches hard lessons. With the swollen federal deficit pushing the limits of even the Congress, environmentally interested taxpayers can expect to find federal dollars for environmental cleanup and management scarce. As interest on the federal deficit consumes ever larger proportions of the federal budget, cuts in other forms of spending become not only necessary but inevitable. These cuts already include the Environmental Protection Agency, overbur-

Left: Makahiki ceremony at sunset, Island of Kaho'olawe. Right: Sun creates a circular rainbow as it shines through the tiny ice particles of high cirrus.

© Franco Salmoiraghi

dened, understaffed, and for the last decade undermined by political considerations. The new scarcity will force us to make choices that reveal anew how we value nature, and whether we can realistically expect our government to have one arm that devastates nature and another that repairs it. In the coming scarcity we will see a struggle to redefine the idea of defense, of what, from what. We will see if it lies within us to call a truce in our war with nature. And in Hawai'i we will watch closely to see if the face of government is that of the good Dr. Jekyl or the destructive Mr. Hyde.

Bringing Gifts to Paradise

© Marc Schechter

Opposite page: Hiker in lower Waimea Canyon on Kaua'i. While it looks beautiful, this view is of predominantly introduced plants, e.g. the Century Plant and Lantana from Mexico; Guava from South America: Molasses Grass, and many others which make up a "transported landscape."
Below right: Enjoying paradise with a Hawai'i grown South American native fruit in hand.

Maybe there is something about paradise that fires the imagination and moves people to imitate the creator. When you survey the contributions of mankind to Hawai'i, much of what troubles the islands seems to have come from good intentions, from human attempts to create an island world in the image of those who want to inhabit it. Whatever the impulse, a succession of immigrants dating to the original Polynesian voyagers some 2,000 years ago has brought plants, animals, and technologies they felt were essential to paradise. All somehow thought that their gifts would improve on what was here before them, as if the islands were for each an unfinished Eden. Like the original creator, each had a vision of shaping the place in his/her own image. If you will survey the landscape of the Hawaiian islands as the century nears its end,

Below: Axis deer were first introduced to
Moloka'i in 1868, and in 1920 to Lana'i.
In the 1950's they were introduced to Maui
for sport hunting. Everywhere, they
increased and caused extensive damage to
pineapple and native forests, including
the Yellow Hibiscus State Flower and
other endangered plants.
Right: West Kaua'i eroded soils caused by
overgrazing by goats and deer.
Introduced browse resistant
trees replace native ecosystems.

70

you will see a patchwork of the dreams of
those who have come here. It is there in the
stands of ironwood trees, the scrub of strawberry guava spilled along the highlands, and
the cattle grazing the nubs of grass on scarred
slopes. It is there in the mynah bird, the Axis
deer, and the wild pig.

Because human beings rely so heavily on
nature for survival, societies go far toward
defining themselves in the way they draw
from and give back to nature. Thousands of
miles from any other resources, Hawaiians
understood the beauty and necessity of a
balance between human needs and natural
resources. As Herb Kane relates in his book
Voyagers, "There was no word for trade or
merchant in any Polynesian language. Exchange of goods and services was by a system
of reciprocal gift-giving . . . Theirs was an
affluent subsistence economy with a built-in

© David Boynton

© Marc Schechter

© David Boynton

Left: At West Beach, O'ahu, sugar fields on the Ewa coral plain are being developed as subdivisions, resort hotels, and harbors.
Below: The Hawaiian Cotton (Ma'o), useful to plant breeders because of its insect hardiness, is an example of native flora displaced by these developments.
Right: Just two miles from downtown Honolulu, there are still watershed reserves where native forests persist.

sense of sufficiency in which exploitation of resources was discontinued when needs were satisfied." Taking too much would clearly mean not only disrespect for life around them, but a loss of immense beauty and inevitable self-destruction. Although they eliminated significant parts of the dryland and mesic forests on the leeward sides of the islands, each generation of Hawaiians was conscious of the need to pass along to the next the gift of a paradise that could sustain a human presence.

In contrast, the expedition that led Cook to Hawai'i represented part of an ongoing series of mercantile adventures conducted by the Spanish, English, French, Portuguese, and Russians over 300 years. By 1778, many native societies of North and South America had already been ravaged by Western Europeans, people who believed it reasonable to take as much from nature as possible. Until the Hawaiians discovered what mattered to these newcomers, they had no way of knowing that the people who sailed in the great ships were moved by dreams of limitless wealth.

Hawaiians now faced visitors instructed by an Old Testament that told them to "increase, multiply, and subdue the earth." Here were strangers who saw man as completely separated from nature. To Cook, Vancouver, La Perouse, Von Kotzebue, and the other adventurers who followed in Cook's path, Hawai'i was either a place to exploit, or a useful station on their way to exploiting other distant lands and seas. To ensure a welcome, the explorers and traders brought gifts with them, plants and animals that would alter forever the balance of paradise.

What unfolded with the arrival of whalers and missionaries in the first fifty years after Cook's mapping of the Sandwich Islands is a story of the collision of two economic systems. The newcomers came armed with powerful weapons and technologies calculated to give them control. Ravaged by diseases brought by the strangers, Hawaiians quickly understood that survival lay in adaptation, in some form of accommodation to the newcomers' gifts: guns, the written word, and efficient machines made of metal.

Each group struggled to keep what it valued the most, and for the invaders that meant the freedom to pursue taking as much from nature as possible. Under the influence of early traders, Kamehameha and other royalty quickly learned to exploit nature as well. Commanded to do so by the chiefs, Hawaiians took so many sandalwoods from the slopes of Waimea, Hawai'i, that the trees all but vanished. The vast expanse of treeless slopes that now extends down to Kawaihae harbor was once verdant with sandalwood (*ili'ahi*). It vanished in a few short years, from 1820 to 1825, when two to four million pounds a year were shipped out. It took 6,000 trees to fill the hold of one ship, and in search of quick

© John S. Callahan

Left: Many islanders jokingly suggest that the State Bird of modern Hawai'i has become the high rise crane.
Right: The Lotus from Asia is the most ancient of cultivated flowers and has an edible tuber.

74

© Franco Salmoiraghi

wealth, the ali'i (Hawaiian royalty) forced whole villages out to harvest the trees over long hours in the hot sun. Many suffered from malnutrition and exposure, and many died. Inevitably, the workers began destroying young plants to assure themselves of freedom from slavery and a chance at survival. There is no record of what other life forms may have disappeared after losing the shelter of the sandalwoods.

Driven by Queen Ka'ahumanu's declaration that all Hawaiians should read the Bible, Hawaiians attending the early schools of the islands obediently sought literacy. With the spiritual underpinnings of their culture dissolved by the Queen's conversion to Christianity, they learned that the white man's god had given humankind dominion over all the beasts of the field and every living thing. Their own royalty, after all, were selling whole boatloads of sandalwood trees. The tools and goods of the newcomers now began to alter age old patterns of work, education, and family. Slowly but inexorably, some Hawaiians began to adopt the newcomers' attitudes toward nature.

The living gifts brought by the visitors created an impact beyond anyone's imagining. Captain Cook had given the Hawaiians goats when he arrived, and now another British

© Robert B. Goodman

Opposite page: Hereford cattle on the Parker Ranch, one of the largest in America. Cattle are the arch enemy of the Hawaiian forests.
Left and below: This pink flower signals a curtain of doom for the koa forest of upper Hamakua. The Banana Poka Vine (Passiflora) originated in the high Andes, was brought to Hawai'i for ornamental purposes, and escaped to become a scourge in our forests.

77

© Tami Dawson

explorer, George Vancouver, brought cattle in the 1890's. Aware of their potential as food and hides, Kamehameha put a *kapu* on the cattle for ten years, i.e., anyone touching them would be severely punished. By the time another visitor brought horses a decade later, growing numbers of cattle, goats, and now pigs had become feral animals foraging in

Left: Topsoil conservation is crucial to the success of diversified agriculture. As plantations close or abandon the marginal sugar lands, extensive erosion can follow.
Right: Feral goats are eating the bark of this Koki'o tree. Extensive goat damage will kill the tree.
Above: Newcomers may perceive only beauty in this Gulf Fritillary butterfly on Lantana blossoms, but these invaders from Mexico are serious pests on Passion Fruit farms.

island forests. At one point in the 19th century, half of the land mass of the Hawaiian islands was devoted to grazing cattle. Today

the patchwork of plants in Hawai'i still bears testimony to the damage brought by these hooved immigrants, from the Kohala coast of the island of Hawai'i, to the ravaged west end of Moloka'i, to the slopes above Moloa'a on the windward coast of Kaua'i.

By the 1830's plants such as strawberry guava and koa haole had also been introduced, and they found the climate and soil of the islands so accommodating that they crowded out many native plants, becoming major pests. One by one new species arrived in the arms or luggage of well intentioned visitors intent on putting their stamp on paradise. Early Polynesians had cultivated sugar, but in the 1830's huge monocultural crops of it were planted on Kaua'i. As water was engineered for irrigation throughout the islands, tens of thousands of acres were put into pineapple and sugar, devastating habitat for many native species.

Leap forward now to 1890, just prior to the overthrow of the Hawaiian kingdom. From a population of 300,000 to 500,000 Hawaiians at the time of Cook's arrival in 1778, sickness and impoverishment had reduced the total population of the islands to just over 80,000, including numerous immigrants, many of them agricultural workers. Control of land and political power had shifted to a powerful merchant class of Americans, who had demonstrated that the natural resources of the islands could be used to turn a profit. While visitors made the long voyage to see the wonders of Hawai'i, tourism did not yet play a major part in commerce.

Now jump to 1990. In 100 years, the population has multiplied roughly 14 times, leaving the islands to support 1.1 million residents and over 6.5 million visitors a year. The state readies an airport to handle 33 percent more visitors by the year 2,000. Housing tracts have wedged their way out onto the plains and up into the central saddle of Oahu. Huge cargo ships filled with goods from overseas arrive several times a week to feed the population. Oil tankers anchor regularly off Barbers Point to off-load petroleum for airplane fuel, gasoline, and electrical generation. Fifteen thousand visitors a day cross the sea to reach Honolulu International Airport.

This rising human tide inevitably has its impact. Sewage systems regularly overflow and spill into offshore waters. A power outage leaves Oahu crippled for a day, while rolling blackouts trouble the island of Hawai'i. Oahu's freeways and surface streets are jammed with auto traffic, for the island has more cars per mile of road than any other American city. Busses run at capacity during peak traffic hours. A simmering controversy over rapid transit on Oahu flares into a heated political dispute when the city council rejects the system. As the population rises, the struggle to accommodate growth holds the political spotlight. No one seems able to ask the obvious but unspeakable question: how many people can these islands far at sea support?

If Hawai'i's population were to mimic the growth of the last 100 years and over the next century multiply another 14 times, the 1.1 million residents of 1990 would swell to an amazing total of

© Marc Schechter

15,400,000 — not counting visitors, who would by then have trouble imagining the islands as a place to vacation. Oahu alone would have to support 11,740,000 people. With limited water, land, housing, and employment, keeping 12 million people on a single tropic isle would become a continuing but losing exercise in crisis management.

If Hawai'i with 1.1 million people shows signs of pressing at its limits, and 15 million residents sounds impossible, then just what is a realistic and acceptable population for the islands? Suppose predictions of crowding and rising costs lead to new limits on growth and population. In a rosier scenario, Oahu's population multiplies only three times over the

Left: Alewa Heights, one of many developments on the slopes overlooking the city of Honolulu. Above the houses is the famed Kamehameha School.
Below: Construction cranes and highrises at sunset.
Right: Masses of plastic, fishnets, and other floating debris carried by Pacific currents, clutter an isolated beach near the south end of Ni'ihau, the island owned and ranched by the Robinson family.

© John S. Callahan

© David Boynton

© David Franzen

Left: Container ship leaving Honolulu Harbor.
Below: Young Hawaiian dancer in Tahitian costume.
Right: Tropical forest destruction for geothermal development, Island of Hawai'i.
Far right: Anti-geothermal protest at Wao Kele O Puna Rain Forest, Island of Hawai'i.

©Robert B. Goodman

next century. The island now has 2.5 million residents — and a visitor population of 18 million. Would that densely populated an Oahu still mean clear waters, a friendly community, and a beautiful place to visit? Or would it mean water rationing, crowded squalor, tattered remnants of nature, and rare glimpses of beauty? At what point will quantity, the sheer number of people, cause the collapse of the quality of life?

Somehow we continue to evade the central question — the limits of growth. While the economy of Hawai'i relies now on being able to offer over 6.5 million visitors a vibrant and flourishing natural environment, anyone looking at Hawai'i's already battered ecosystems cannot help but come away alarmed. In its September, 1992 issue of *Elepaio*, the Hawai'i Audubon Society offered a convincing case for the spreading devastation of

© G. Brad Lewis

© Franco Salmoiraghi

nature and the ineffectiveness of the Endangered Species Act to prevent further losses: "More than 72% of our nation's historically documented plant and bird extinctions are from Hawaii, as are more than 27% of the currently listed threatened and endangered birds and plants." According to the Hawai'i State Department of Land and Natural Resources, Hawai'i has less than 0.2 % of the total land mass of the U.S., but more than 25% of our country's endangered birds and plant species.

Another perceptive environmental observer, G. Tyler Miller, sees Hawai'i as "fast becoming the world capital of biological extinction because of increasing population and development." Whether it is the arrival here of 20 new alien species a year, the pollution caused by sheer numbers of people in our shoreline waters, or the quiet extinction of the Moloka'i Creeper, the signs tell us that the gifts we have brought to paradise now threaten to sink it.

Those who believe that environmental losses hold no real significance for the economy remain lost in yesterday's dream. Though it relies on its beaches to attract tourists, Oahu has lost nine miles of sandy beaches in the last 65 years, and beach enlargement at Waikiki has been needed twice in the last 30 years. Moreover, Oahu remains over 90% dependent on imported oil to generate electricity. Recent oil spills in Oahu's waters suggest the possibility of a larger spill that could sweep down upon Oahu's reefs and tourist beaches. As if to confirm this concern, a group of 41 oil transport and drilling firms has invested $70 million in an oil spill cleanup facility scheduled to open in the summer of 1993 some 50 miles above Los Angeles. Amid the applause for such responsible preparation, it is chilling to note that the center is preparing to handle

Below: Torch Ginger, an imported ornamental which has not yet established itself in the wild.
Right: Kahili Ginger, an import from the Himalayas has established itself in the wild, infesting National Parks and other remote forests. No island insects are able to keep it in balance.
Lower right: Jenna, age 7, North Shore, O'ahu.

© Jaime Wellner

oil spills in both California and Hawai'i.

At the 1992 conference on tourism and the environment in Honolulu, everything went as expected. Environmental experts issued clear warnings about overreaching the limits of nature's resiliency. Proponents of tourism listened thoughtfully, espoused the causes of recycling and environmental protection, and

as expected, went on dreaming of growth. Although all recognize that many of the remaining flora and fauna of the islands are vanishing, no one seems willing to believe that the declining environment has limits. If we allow nature to collapse piece by piece around us, we may then witness a collapse of the tourist-driven economy from which the islands may never recover.

Early visitors to Hawai'i could not have foreseen that the gifts they brought would begin to unbalance the ecosystem that had developed long before their arrival. We, however, have the benefit of sophisticated environmental science, and with it better vision that leaves us few excuses for destroying what we have. Our controversies over transit, sewage, highways, development, and energy all mask the larger questions of acceptable limits to our population and acceptable losses in nature. Ironically, we now can see that if we continue to shape paradise in our own image, we will destroy the paradise that so many of us hope to enjoy.

The Paradise Index

© Jack Jeffrey

Left: With 460 inches of rain yearly, the summit above Kaua'i's Alaka'i Swamp was Earth's wettest spot until upstaged by a town in North India with 467 inches of yearly rain.
Above: Delicious edible fruit of 'Ohelo (Vaccinium), a member of the Cranberry family, is sacred to Pele, the Volcano Goddess.

For most people measurements of economic phenomena read like road signs in a foreign alphabet. They create a kind of economic shamanism that leaves economists nodding knowingly, while the unanointed simply wonder what all the mumbo-jumbo is about. When you look at them a little more closely, even the economic measurements you hear on the evening news or see in *Time* magazine suffer from a substantial number of omissions, flaws, and biases. They generally include quantities, i.e., how much we are producing, how many people need work, or how many houses have been built, and they imply that if you can quantify something, you have the best chance of understanding it. Quantities yield patterns, and patterns may suggest what will happen next, so economists eventually combined some of their measurements into what they call Leading Economic

Indicators. However valuable this index may be, smart business people still read between the lines in the daily news and watch what people put in their shopping carts.

Because of the difficulties in measuring it, the quality of life often goes unmeasured and usually doesn't appear in the equations of economists. While we have some figures on homelessness and consumer confidence, we don't know much about (and therefore don't pay much attention to) the inner landscapes of our people, the fear, hopelessness, joy, and general confidence we feel in our lives. Moreover, we hear only anecdotes about damage to nature caused by our economic way of life. A well may turn up with pesticides in it, or a toxic spill may threaten a town or a shoreline; it takes a crisis to put nature in the news. But when something puts a part of nature in danger, news coverage focuses on health hazards, property rights, Hawaiian rights, or zoning. All are important concerns, but they cloud a larger, long term issue. Biological systems keep us alive every bit as much as economic systems, yet when it comes to information

© David Boynton

Above: Conservation biologist Steven Montgomery studying the pollinators of a delicate native mint (Haplostachys), known solely from the Big Island's dry central saddle lands.

© Jack Jeffrey

© Jack Jeffrey

© G. Brad Lewis

Above: The Silversword population of Mauna Kea, Hawai'i is slowly recovering from a century of browsing by feral sheep.
Center: Haha (Clermontia) is a large lobelia. Its flowers are normally horizontal, aiding the birds which help pollinate it in exchange for nectar.
Right: 'Ama'u fern (see p.26) has a red pigment to protect the young fronds from the strong sunlight at high elevations.

© Steven Lee Montgomery

about the biological system, other news crowds it out. Perhaps a deeper reason for our ignorance of nature lies in what we lack. In a world where we seem able to measure and report almost anything, we have no systematic way of measuring what is happening to island ecosystems, much less any consistent, understandable way to let the public know about them.

The need for measuring nature became an issue when it began to intrude in events like the toxic fog in London in the 1950's that killed people, and in the alarms about pesticides set off by Rachel Carson in her 1962 classic *Silent Spring*. In recent times biological measurement has achieved quantum leaps. On the microcosmic scale we can now determine the parts per million of pesticides in ground water, and we can discover in intimate detail the genetic structure of living

© Kenneth M. Nagata

Above: Back in 1909, when it was first discovered by Joseph Rock at Puu Waʻawaʻa, this Kokiʻo, or tree cotton, was already a rarity due to goat and cattle feeding. Today, only a dozen are known.
Left: The state flower is the dry climate Hibiscus (H. brackenridgei), known to Hawaiians as Maʻo Hau Hele. It too is an endangered plant.

Above: The Uhiuhi tree has ebony-colored wood and seeds so dense that they sink in water. Hawaiians used its wood extensively as bait sticks for fishing. The Uhiuhi is now endangered by overgrazing and fires in North Kona.

© David Boynton

things. On the macrocosmic scale, we have satellites tracing the flow of the world's weather, instruments measuring the intensity of UV rays entering the earth's atmosphere, and ways to determine the annual loss of topsoil worldwide. We now talk globally about the Gaia Thesis and Chaos Theory, and universally about the Theory of Everything. Ironically, on a group of islands with limited land space, we still lack a comprehensive system for measuring the health of the eco-systems that support us.

Scientists and foresters already gather some useful data, which appears piecemeal in environmental newsletters and some government reports. So I propose that we close this gap with a new form of measure-ment. Call it the Paradise Index, for it can provide all of us with a way of knowing if the biological system of the Hawaiian Islands is thriving, what the human presence is doing to it, and what we may expect from nature in the future. From the information the Index regularly presents, we could gain a different sense of the quality of our lives as a part of the larger ecosystem which we share with all the life forms around us.

The Paradise Index would arrive as a kind of "Leading Economic Indicators" for the environment. It would assign weight to a list of various biological measurements which we know are important, then put them into a single index. First it would establish a series of critical eco-regions that are needed for the support of the essential resident species of the islands, including human beings. These valu-able eco-regions would allow the islands to retain not only their natural character, but their long term habitability by their resident species (again including human beings, where appropriate). In these eco-areas, a more lim-ited Native Paradise Index would measure:

— the diversity, health and balance of resident plant life
— the population, health and balance of resident animal species
— water availability and quality
— new floral and animal pests introduced
— habitat available for native plants, and habitat at risk
— species at risk or endangered
— other indices of the biological system's vigor.

The Native Paradise Index would give us a regularly updated look at the biosystem we must preserve for the long run.

Incorporating information from the Native Paradise Index, the statewide Paradise Index would then measure:

— water quality in aquifers, streams and at beaches
— air quality
— energy use per capita
— population density and population
— visitor traffic
— sewage and landfill volume and their quality control
— vehicles in the state
— CO2 and sulfur dioxide emissions
— traffic congestion
— crop damage from pests and pesticides
— topsoil loss
— human disease rates/deaths attributable to environmental damage
— trash produced per person
— rainfall by region
— water consumption vs. water availability
— and so forth.

Naturally we would need an island-by-island breakdown of the data to allow each island to establish standards below which the index could not fall without changes in human behaviors contributing to the problems.

Left: At South Point on the Island of Hawai'i, salt spray nurtures the succulent, delicate endangered Portulaca villosa.
Right: The montane forests of the Big Island are the only home of the increasingly rare 'Akiapola'au, Hawai'i's extraordinary version of the woodpecker. The lower bill can chisel into wood, then the flexible upper bill probes to extract a grub.

© Jack Jeffrey

93

For example, if water quality at a given beach fell, and non-point source runoff was the assignable cause, then recreational uses, the use of pesticides, faulty septic tanks, and droppings from pets draining into that area would have to be dealt with differently.

Such a system would probably require measurements around the state to set up a baseline biennial measurement of environmental quality for each island and its offshore waters. Fortunately we have a number of models to draw on where data from satellite photographs has been combined with data from earth-bound sources to establish comprehensive data bases of ecosystems and rare species. The Nature Conservancy in Arlington, Virginia, for example, maintains its Biological and Conservation Data System with such satellite information. New lightweight tracking devices (less than an ounce) also allow biologists to track the movements of endangered species. Combining satellite imagery, computers, data bases and tracking devices with data from trained biologists

© Jack Jeffrey

Left: The Crested Honeycreeper ('Akohekohe) favors nectar from 'Ohi'a Lehua blossoms, and is the only native bird with a fuzzy tuft. The first nest of the endangered species was discovered in 1992 in the Waikamoi Preserve, managed by the Nature Conservancy.
Below: The endangered 'Akepa frequents the forest canopy, where it pries open leaf buds for insects.

© David Boynton

already working in the field, Hawai'i should be able to establish a sophisticated measurement of our essential ecosystems.

The state (perhaps combining the Hawaii Visitors Bureau, the Department of Land and Natural Resources, the visitor industry, and non-profit environmental organizations) would first have to determine the cost of such a program, then have to make a commitment to fund Paradise Index measurements. Once the baseline measurements were in place, we would be able to measure scientifically the gains and losses of environmental quality.

Naturally there will be opposition to this new approach from those who have a major stake in things as they are. The eco-regions of the islands will certainly cross the boundaries of privately and publicly controlled lands. Some private land owners may balk at having their flora and fauna measured, for a closer look may reveal the environmental damage being done by their uses of the land. State leases of land, particularly those of Hawaiian Homestead land, will also come into scrutiny

© Tami Dawson

and create some discomfort. Clearly we will have to come up with a system of incentives (and perhaps penalties) for private landholders to use their land wisely. Whatever the political headwinds that would hold back the Paradise Index, the signals from nature already tell us that we will need accurate scientific measurements of the biosystem if we hope to make sensible decisions about protecting it.

Many state laws already require the state to fulfill Article XI of the Hawai'i State Constitution, which directs the state to "conserve and protect Hawai'i's . . . natural resources." In a 1988 plan, the State Division of Forestry and Wildlife published its intention to identify the needs of threatened and endangered species, but since the plan, native species have continued their tragic decline. Hawai'i has 108,000 acres (18 reserves on five islands) as the state

© Jack Jeffrey

Natural Area Reserves System. But if the NARS represents a laudable idea, in practice the protection of these and other large areas controlled by the state has fallen short, as the state's own publication (*Why We Must Preserve Hawai'i's Natural Treasures*) relates:

Upper left: Even at nature preserves like Mo'omomi Dunes, invading all-terrain-vehicles threaten to smash coastal plants like the endangered 'Ohai, a prostrate shrub in the pea family.
Above: The Palila is a finch-billed honeycreeper known only from the high Mamane forests of the Big Island where Mamane tree seed pods supply its main food.
Right: At Kaua'i's Hawai'i Plant Conservation Center, a horticulturist cares for seedlings of an endangered species.

"Hawai'i's unique natural inheritance is the most critically endangered in the U.S."

Our environment is the primary asset we offer to visitors, and it is the only nature we have to support residents. Ironically, the state of Hawai'i presently devotes less than one-tenth of one percent of its total budget to the Division of Environmental Management, which monitors the quality of air, water, and land in the islands. In this light, the Paradise Index appears less like an expensive science fiction and more like a necessity that doubles as a good business investment. Beyond moving the state's priorities toward conservation, the Index would give businesses in the islands something unique to brag about — a place where people care so much about the quality of nature and natural beauty that we measure it regularly and set limits on its losses. Imagine how good we would feel about this legacy for our children.

By making the Paradise Index a highly publicized matter of public record every two years, we would establish standards of what nature must have to do to sustain its essential systems. We would also, as a society, make a public statement about what we value in nature. Such a system would also help us make better long term economic choices, and it might foster the environmental consciousness we see emerging among our children and some governmental and business leaders. Finally, the Paradise Index would make these environmental standards a matter of public accountability by area, and in turn make them an issue in every contest for elective public office. With the measurement of our island ecosystems and their new public importance, the Paradise Index could become an environmental model for every community.

© John S. Callahan

How to Stay in Paradise

Every society struggles to answer an enduring question, one which shapes the destiny of its people. Put simply, the issue is this: at what point does the pursuit of self-interest have to give way to the pursuit of what is good for the community?

Globally, nationally, and in Hawai'i, the environmental costs of self-interest bear remarkable similarities. Humanity is presently adding roughly 95 million people a year to the 5.45 billion the earth now struggles to support. Every two years and eight months, we add to the total as many people as now live in the United States. At current growth rates, the human population of the world will reach 11 billion people in just thirty-five years. As you

© G. Brad Lewis

Left: H-1 Freeway, afternoon rush hour traffic.
Right: Young man with ukulele and white orchid.

Above: Only on the remote Northwestern Hawaiian Islands, and Ni'ihau, does the endangered Hawaiian Monk Seal find respite from the 1,100,000 primates now inhabiting the main islands. Right: Anahola, Kaua'i. One of three temporary dumping sites after Hurricane Iniki. The storm created the equivalent of 15 years of trash in one day.

can imagine, amid this kind of amazing exponential growth, the sheer number of people pursuing self-interest inevitably collides with the limits of what nature can sustain.

In the United States, the individual's fundamental right to pursue a materially better way of life remains an article of faith in the American Dream, but the addition of each new American makes ever greater demands on natural resources. Compared to the average citizen of the planet, the average American consumes five times as much energy and produces twice as much garbage. It should come as no surprise that Americans also have the highest number of cars per capita in the world, and that the number of miles we drive has doubled since 1970. If we have concerns about the good of community, we need to look at how self-interest transforms into unchecked growth that in turn carries rising environmental costs.

Hawai'i offers a useful microcosm of what others can expect to encounter as they watch their growth reach the limits of nature. In the last 40 years, as Florida, Arizona, California, and rest of the American sunbelt have swelled with people, the population of Hawai'i has doubled. While we have enjoyed the economic growth, we have also struggled to keep up with demand for sewers, highways, air-

ports, and schools to accommodate a rising population. Caught up in pursuing a rising standard of living, we have ignored nature and have unconsciously slipped into defining the "good of the community" as "more for everyone materially." In Hawai'i, for example, we now have 170 persons per square mile (versus 70 per square mile nationally). We have nearly as many vehicles as we have people, .8 of one for each resident. But as we have added buildings, roads, cars, businesses, and solid waste landfills to sustain our population, the environment has moved steadily toward collapse. With the surrounding sea to remind us of the finite limits of frail island resources, unchecked self-interest begins to sound a lot less appealing.

In the last decade, news of global warming, ozone depletion, declining aquifers, and destruction of forests has led to a new definition of the word *community*. With nature imperiled on a grand scale, we are now called on to see *community* not simply as a gathering of human beings, but as the community of all living things. Across America the spirit of the times shows a rising interest in the good of this *community*. Major national corporations have begun to see that environmental consciousness serves the profit motive, and they have begun subscribing to green rules of design, production, and waste disposal. *Fortune* magazine recently sponsored a major national conference to foster business support for the environment. Major computer makers have created new processes to cut down on their uses of chloroflourocarbons. Even venerable McDonalds has moved to hamburgers in brown paper bags and to serious recycling of paper wastes.

As they have nationally, smart business people in Hawai'i see the practical wisdom and the profit in recycling wastes, conserving energy, and protecting green areas. The restaurant and visitor industries have led the way. Outrigger Hotels, Hilton Hawaiian Village, the Aston Hotels and Resorts, and the Kapalua Resort on Maui have won awards for recycling, energy conservation, and protection of native habitat. Visitor destinations such as the Lodge at Ko'ele and the Manele Bay Hotel on Lanai have even leased land to the Nature Conservancy of Hawai'i to ensure

Left: Ho'i'o fern. Wild pigs love to eat the young tips. Right: Sea cliffs at Pololu Valley, North Kohala coast of the Island of Hawai'i.

103

the protection of local wildlife. On the island of Hawai'i, the Mauna Kea Beach Resort carefully engineered construction of the Hapuna golf course to use native grasses exclusively. The result is a course that has state-of-the-art computerized irrigation that monitors rainfall, wind, and sunshine, cutting water use by 350,000 gallons per day. In another encouraging trend, business startups have recently made eco-tourism a possibility for visitors who long to see Hawai'i's nature untrammeled.

Ecological manufactures and merchants have appeared as well. Some have observed the irony of Hawai'i importing all of its soil amendment and paying to put organic waste into landfill as garbage. In response they have created startups in composting on Kaua'i, Maui, and Oahu. On the island of Hawai'i, one entrepreneur has funding for a solar car startup, and in Honolulu EarthWare, the first retailer specializing in environmentally conscious products, is now open for business. Over 60,000 homes now use the abundant sun of the islands for solar water heating, their owners taking advantage of the state's 35% solar tax credit. The future of businesses like these may hinge on the responsiveness of state and county offices, which can obstruct them with red tape or encourage them with sensible rules and advocacy of new legislation to smooth their way.

Above left: Waikaloa golf course, Island of Hawai'i.
Above right: Solar panels, Honolulu.

More encouraging signs lie in the work of organizations like the Conservation Council of Hawai'i, The Nature Conservancy of Hawai'i, the Sierra Club Legal Defense Fund, the Natural Resources Defense Council, Recycle Hawai'i, the City and County of Honolulu's faltering start on serious recycling, and a long list of national and local non-profit environmental activist groups who see paradise in need of protection. Many business people and concerned ordinary citizens find in these organizations alternatives for turning concern into action. The Nature Conservancy's Corporate Council for the Environment, for example, includes among its growing list of subscribing businesses most of the major corporations in the state. As one local CEO has put it, "Here in Hawai'i, even more than in other place across the globe, we cannot afford to take the environment for granted."

Government agencies that we have expected to protect the environment now show signs of waking from a long slumber. The undermanned and politically compromised federal Environmental Protection Agency and the new White House Office of Environmental Policy promise to create a new sense of mission with environmentalist Al Gore as Vice President. After years of an underbudgeted struggle to monitor health risks in the islands, the Hawai'i State Department of Health now

Above left: Shredded plastic for recycling, Island of Hawai'i.
Above: Kahua Ranch wind farm, Island of Hawai'i.

106

advocates pricing demands made on the environment by taxing water use, effluent discharges, hazardous waste storage, and other environmental demands on state services. These funds would replace the tiny budget allocation currently in place and pay for monitoring and regulation of air, water, and ground quality. Because they tax users and focus on costs otherwise lost in the general budget, they would also draw needed attention to the real costs of population and growth. It is essential, however, that these user fees be substantial enough to allow more thorough, frequent, and sophisticated environmental measurements. And as if to keep up with the times, even the City and County of Honolulu has plans to expand its recycling program.

These attempts to limit the damage of a consumer culture on small islands give all of us reasons for hope. But beyond pursuing damage control in a growth-oriented society, what would it take (in the best of all possible worlds) to move us from where we now are —

still pursuing growth — to where we might question or limit growth itself? What kind of considerations might be involved in setting practical limits on growth? What would the political and economic landscape look like as we shifted toward a sustainable, non-growth economy in Hawai'i?

Clearly limiting growth would bring political heavy weather and economic dislocations, and so far our political leaders have balked at advocating anything so controversial. As it has in many communities blessed with abundant sun, the construction industry has become a significant source of jobs and income in Hawai'i. Land owners and existing businesses have come to expect that growth will increase the value of their holdings. Even the state government is betting on economic expansion as it invests several billion dollars in a new freeway and an enlargement of Honolulu International Airport. The once sleepy islands of Hawai'i are clearly hooked on growth.

Over the last 200 years, self-interest has developed into an unquestioned economic article of faith. To question self-interest and

growth is to question what allows individuals to pursue their dreams. Supporting more people brings business and government their power, and theoretically this growth enlarges the possibility for each of us to have more materially. But it is this very fixation on *more* in conventional thinking that leaves us with too many people using too much, more calls for government intervention, and greater damage to the natural environment. It takes almost no imagination to see the self-destructive consequences which the pursuit of *more* will bring us, yet we seem unable to conceive of limiting numbers of people and our demands on natural resources. While business leaders and elected officials sign up with environmental organizations, none seems willing to address in concrete terms the underlying but obvious question: just how much growth can our fragile islands sustain?

Ironically, distress signals from the environment show us that we have already had too much success in realizing our material

108

Left: These cliffs on Kaua'i's Na Pali Coast have been carved by five million years of wind and rain.

dreams. Zoning litigation, disputes over increasing sewage spills, disagreements over rapid transit, and the housing shortage — all are the consequences of too many people achieving their dreams, then expecting still more. Now, in the early 1990's, our collective ability to realize our dreams poses a challenge, for in their aggregate our personal dreams have the potential to destroy what each of us wants.

To begin putting limits on growth would mean reshaping the deepest assumptions of our society. Our attitudes about property ownership, individual freedoms, and our personal expectations would have to shift away from self and toward what benefits the *community*. If that sounds a bit dreamy and utopian, remember that nature is already beginning to show us the real numbers of people that island ecosystems can reasonably accommodate. Given our current course, biology will eventually collide with the economics of growth, and in the long run, economics will certainly lose.

Toward putting the limits of growth into the arena of public discussion, I offer the following modest proposals for change.

— Create an amendment to the state constitution that would establish the goal of a sustainable economy with limits to growth and population, and protection of essential habitat for all native species. Hawai'i's state motto reads, "The life of the land is preserved in righteousness." Let's put the state motto into operation in the state constitution and state law.
—Establish an environmental master plan. On the basis of scientific study (publicly funded, but conducted by independent sources), a panel representing industry, the public, government, and environmental groups would establish the critical warning species in Hawai'i, the island equivalents of the spotted owl of the Northwest. Next they would determine critical eco-regions, as the U.S. Fish and Wildlife Service and the Hawaii Department of Fish and Wildlife have begun studying. Beyond establishing these eco-regions, however, the state would also have to set population goals, and would have to set what we consider acceptable environmental losses, designating on every island those regions which are absolutely essential as habitat for native species and for our water table.
—To assure their protection, these ecological master plan lands/waters would have new limitations put on their use, limitations well beyond those that accompany zoning them as parks, agricultural zones, or watershed. Many such lands and waters, for example, would essentially operate as nature preserves. Over

© David Boynton

Left: Green Iguana captured at Anahola, Kaua'i. Because these lizards pose a threat to flowering plants, they are prohibited entry as pets.
Below: Brown tree snake of Asia, not established in Hawai'i, but responsible for exterminating many of Guam's native birds as well as frequently shorting out the electric grid. Individual tree snakes have entered Hawai'i via the wheel wells and cargo of U.S. Air Force transports. Fortunately, they have been dead on arrival.

a long period of investment, the state or non-profit environmental groups would acquire and care for such lands. At the same time, the state would also double the tax deductions of those contributing to designated private organizations which create and maintain such preserves. It would also give private landowners strong tax incentives to protect endangered species and native ecosystems identified on their property. Finally, the state would offer major tax incentives and assistance to those who would take agricultural lands out of sugar and use them to plant produce for local consumption.

— Move island species from the waiting list onto the Endangered Species List now.

© Gordon Rodda

— Stop the arrival of alien pests. Recently introduced cannibal snails are devouring native snails species rapidly, and one voracious newcomer, the Argentine ant, destroys pollinators and alters the food chain. Alien grasses, such as fountain grass and molasses grass, were introduced between 1920 and 1970 and have choked out native species and made forest fires far more likely. On a more frightening note, in the last ten years local authorities have discovered everything from a boa constrictor and a cayman to piranha fish, lending urgency to the need for stricter controls.

We need to reshape the appropriate state and federal government agencies into an effective force, as proposed in the Hawaiian Native Ecosystem Act now before Congress. The background and sensible guidelines that can make this happen are already suggested in The Nature Conservancy/Natural Resources Defense Council 1992 report, *The Alien Pest Species Invasion of Hawai'i.* With five state, five federal, and eight private agencies trying to deal just with alien pests,

clearly it is time to unify our efforts to make sure we stem the flow of pests that damage our agriculture and put native habitat at risk. Fortunately a proposed new federal law will allow postal service employees to investigate Hawai'i-bound mail for alien plants and animals. It also makes it easier for state and federal agencies to work together in halting the influx of alien species.
— Update and revise Hawai'i's own endangered species act with standards much more stringent than those of the federal act of 1973 now awaiting renewal.
— Establish a comprehensive system for measuring the quality of eco-regions, using satellite mapping, new tracking devices, and the field scientists of both public and private agencies. This approach would develop the maps now used by the Office of State Planning into the regularly measured *Paradise Index,* which will relate in detail and by area how the environment is faring under mankind's stewardship. Under a state contract and a MacArthur Foundation grant, The Nature Conservancy has the beginnings of just such a project. The Hawai'i Conservation

© David Boynton

Above: Arborist Ken Wood has discovered over 20 new plants, many on these goat-free cliffs in Kalalau Valley, Kaua'i.

Left: The Ili'au (Wilkesia) is a West Kaua'i relative of the Silversword that blossoms in May after years of growth, seeds, and then dies. Eight feet in height is not uncommon.

© David Boynton

Biology Initiative will begin taking first steps to coordinate ecological research in Hawai'i.

I propose that once *The Paradise Index* is in place, the state should require and fund biennial publication of the information with large ads in the daily papers and presentations on statewide public television. Let us become the first state to advertise to the world how much we care for the natural wonders of the islands. To make sure that the current hodge podge of overlapping state agencies no longer can ignore enforcement of environmental laws, I propose that we create an elected, statewide Environmental Monitoring Group with the power to penalize those (including state and county governments) failing to observe limitations on critical eco-regions. A new state Environmental Protection Agency would carry out its directives.

— Fund development of the environmental master plan through startup grants that set a plan in place by a deadline. Fund operation of the plan through dedicated state environmental taxes on construction, water use, effluent discharge, solid waste disposal, gasoline, and car licenses. Federal law now pushes utilities producing CO_2 to buy pollution credits for emissions beyond a standard linked to their previous emissions. Hawai'i needs to broaden that perspective by attaching the costs of environmental cleanup as closely as possible to all those who create pollution. What I propose is expensive, but given that we have only one besieged environment to sustain us, we have to see these measures as common sense investments in our future.

— Islands have visible limits, and we can see elsewhere what overpopulation can do to them. On one atoll in the Marshall chain, 12,000 people live in crowded squalor on 91 acres, an area roughly that of Kapiolani Park in Honolulu.

Our own population growth already faces limits, probably sooner than we expect, but certainly for the grandchildren of those now in our schools. Rather than pretending that we can grow endlessly, then suddenly realizing we are in trouble, we must take a bold path toward limiting the population of the future.

About 2% of island residents migrate elsewhere each year because of crowding, the high cost of living, or poor economic prospects. Still, Hawai'i's ratio of births and immigrants to deaths leaves our population growing steadily at 2% a year. Because it will take some years to alter the demographic vector of births, we need to make changes now. If we do not, nature and economics eventually will force us to accept not just losses of visitors, but a rapid decline in the quality of life and the serious social problems that attend crowding.

The first essential step will probably raise controversies about reproductive freedom, constitutional guarantees, regressive taxation, and even cultural bias, but we need to become the first state with legislation that changes tax incentives toward limiting population growth.

Over the next 20 years, we should gradually end tax deductions beyond one child per parent, i.e., tax deductions for one child per natural parent would remain, but tax breaks for additional children would be phased out over 20 years. In their place we would introduce over the subsequent 20 years gradual tax penalties for children beyond one per parent. Over 40 years people would have to get accustomed to the reality of paying as much in additional taxes as they once used to save by having a third or fourth child. Young people growing into child-bearing years would have to confront the social consequences of reproduction, acknowledging

Below: A young girl practicing with poi balls for a New Zealand Maori women's dance. A strong bond exists between native Hawaiians and their Maori Polynesian cousins.

114

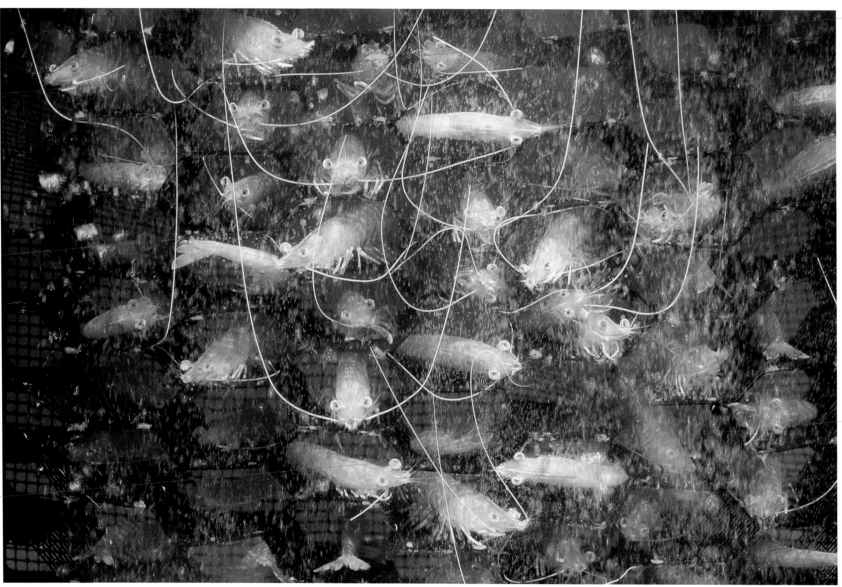

© Robert B. Goodman

what their ancestors of the 1990's did not, that paradise has both a price and real limits.

As for immigrants to the state, the U.S. Constitution makes it impossible to halt people from choosing to live here, but the new tax disincentives could act as a deterrent, with the continuing steep cost of living serving the same purpose.

As we near the limits of our natural resources, we have to recognize that a total state population of even as few as 2.5 million (roughly double the present numbers) would create terrific demands on sewers, schools, roads, public services, and natural resources. Before we push nature toward a still steeper decline, we need public policies that confront the limits of population.

– To fulfill the new science requirement recently instituted by the Board of Education (but unfunded by the legislature), require a new course in all secondary schools that examines ecosystems, population, and economics. The aim of such a course would be to

Left: Shrimp condo at the University of Hawai'i Hawai'i Institute of Marine Biology on Coconut Island. Scientists experimented with raising shrimp for market where each shrimp had its own little apartment and needed only to eat, sleep, drink and grow fat. A couch shrimp. It failed!
Right center: Na'ena'e (Dubautia) on lichen covered lava.

help young people address the impact of population growth on their own lives, the economy, the ecosystem, and island society.

We would need to create a similar course as a graduation requirement for community colleges and for all branches of the University of Hawai'i. It would also become a university credit course required of all teachers. Next we

© Jack Jeffrey

should fund a public television series to present the same subject via broadcast to adults in the community. This course should include the ecological master plan of the islands, a close look at natural resources and environmental pressures, field trips to observe the species at risk and real evidence of widespread environmental damage. It would also need to examine what continuing eco-damage

will mean for larger resident human populations and future visitors. Economic, social, environmental, and political arguments for and against growth should have full airing in this course. The subject of the limits of growth should become the central issue of ongoing discussion in Hawaii.

— Increase scientific research and training focused on Hawaii's conservation challenges. Fund a large corp of summer interns and graduate students to work in the field with experienced scientists on everything from water quality to conserving habitat. The University of Hawai'i at Manoa has just made a wonderful step in that direction, introducing a new graduate program that offers a specialty in a combination of ecology, evolution, and conservation biology.

— Conserve. Via state laws encouraging conservation and investments in the environment, limit, then cut our CO_2 and other greenhouse gas emissions. Introduce a public/private program that plants native species and other flora appropriate to elevation and climate. Current programs fall far short of keeping up with the additional C02 and the other greenhouse gas emissions that our growth produces, i.e., we are net polluters of our own and the world's air quality, and we contribute to global warming.

Institute fast-track integrated resource planning for all electrical producers in the state, moving them to encourage conservation measures among their customers while maintaining their profit base. For example, provide a one-time-only tax credit for all who replace traditional incandescent bulbs with new low energy lighting equivalents. Southern California Edison Company has met most of its additional power demands via conservation for a decade, and meanwhile we, who rely almost entirely on outside energy sources, lack such incentives and continue to build generating capacity. Our Public Utilities Commission is only now considering giving electrical utilities incentives to push conservation.

Add requirements to the building code for solar panels and solar water heating on all residential construction.

Instead of waiting for federal laws to mandate increased car mileage, raise state taxes on gasoline at the pump to provide incentives for cars to get better mileage. We also need tougher smog laws and better enforcement of same. Finally, we need to use tax incentives as well to encourage the use of alternate forms of energy for vehicles and energy efficient appliances.

— Hawai'i's legislators at the federal level should work to cut back military bases on a regular schedule to reach the minimal limit of what defense of the U.S. needs. The military brings $3.5 billion a year to the island economy, a leftover from WWII and the Cold War. The longer we rely on this federal money, the less willing we will be to develop our own diversified, more self-sufficient economy. As we face massive federal deficits, military monies for Hawai'i will surely shrink as the military budget shrinks. Instead of waiting for a budget cut to surprise us, we must start now to plan a transition and a more diversified economy.

— Insist on federal expenditure of funds from the Defense Environmental Restoration Program (DERP) and the Environmental Protection Agency to cleanup military toxic waste sites now on both federal military sites and private land leased to the military for training. We have over 200 such sites in the islands. Tolerate no more delays. Use the Freedom of Information Act to discover all sites in island waters presently contaminated by the military and any others with toxic and nuclear wastes. Establish an ongoing program of cleanup of these sites wherever possible, with independent civilian oversight accountable to the state and to the public.

— Create a new Hawaiian GreenSeal Organization whose environmental values local businesses can develop, espouse, and practice, advertising their affiliation to their customers who can reward them with business. The seeds of such an organization already exist in The Nature Conservancy's statewide Corporate Council for the Environment. Member businesses might join in sales promotions where a small part of profits fund tree plantings or protection of native habitat. To make sure that environmental values they subscribe to actually operate among these

Right: Carnivorous Mikinalo sun dew plant (Drosera anglica) grows in Kaua'i bogs. Sticky droplets on hairs catch small insects.

businesses, set up an arbitration board with representatives from business, environmental organizations, government, and citizens to hear complaints. Publicize both the tree plantings and the consequences of arbitration. Create an intensive, long term media and educational campaign with public service announcements and ongoing educational packages for children and adults regarding responsibility for the environment. Hawaiian Electric Company has introduced just such an educational package that has students and parents assess their energy uses and find where they can conserve. Other companies and institutions such as the Department of Land and Natural Resources should join the Department of Education and private educational institutions to create more such packages. Offer small tax incentives for radio and TV stations carrying these environmental protection messages as a public service. Environmental groups here would be able to join a consortium of all local media sources to contribute to a pool providing environmental expertise, production talent and equipment, and broadcast time.

— We are running short of landfill space for our island consumer society. Institute a statewide law covering: a) significant refunds for all glass, plastic, and aluminum beverage containers, following the lead of the long-proven Oregon container law; b) establish additional taxes on packaging and containers of consumer items that must be put into land fill. Drive up the prices on these kinds of packaging to discourage their import or their use here, and use the money from these taxes to fund other environmental efforts. While some now see H-Power as an answer to ridding ourselves of burnable containers, H-Power is a money-losing proposition that encourages the import of throw-away packaging.

In the absence of a container law, offer tax incentives for the collection of glass and for paving contractors who use it as glasscrete and glassphalt wherever appropriate for paving.
— Make public transportation convenient and attractive, and private transportation expensive. Create on every island a first class bus system, with buses that can run on natural gas along high speed lanes on highways, and jitneys that can provide urban areas with frequent service to link with trunk lines. Institute staggered work hours and school hours. Tax downtown parking on Oahu. Raise car license fees and gasoline taxes gradually over a decade to help pay for the system.
— Plant native trees which encourage biodiversity, lots of them. Reforestation efforts in the islands for years favored recently introduced tree species, because such trees grew easily, protected watershed, and had future commercial value. In fact, it was principally state economic subsidies and widespread knowledge of how to propagate them that led to their planting.

Now evidence indicates that pines and eucalyptus, for example, maintain monocultures that suppress other plant growth. Moreover, their prices per board foot cannot compete with those of native hardwoods. Beyond their commercial advantages, native koa, 'ohi'a, and sandalwood allow for far greater biodiversity, which in turn creates habitat for native creatures and a place for understory native plants. The latter, plants such as hapu'u tree ferns, ferns, and maile, have economic value as well. Fortunately propagation of native species has improved considerably in recent times.

With the arrival of the Hawai'i Tropical Forest Recovery Act, the islands have the potential to become an international showcase for regenerating native forests. Senator Daniel Akaka, who sponsored the law, feels that it will put "ailing tropical forests... on the road to recovery, restoring the health of these

© David Boynton

Left: Large Koa tree.
Below: Behold but beware of the deadly
Amanita poisonous mushrooms that
spring up under the Loblolly Pine tree
plantations in West Kaua'i's Puu Ka Pele
Forest Reserve.

© David Boynton

critical habitats." Joining five federal appointees on The Hawai'i Tropical Forest Recovery Task Force are six local representatives: Rick Scudder of the Conservation Council for Hawai'i; Kelvin Taketa of The Nature Conservancy; Kenneth Kaneshiro of the University of Hawai'i; J.W.A. "Doc" Buyers of C. Brewer; and two representatives from the Hawai'i Department of Land and Natural Resources, Keith Ahue and Charles Wakida.

No one among us knows how a mainstream western consumer society can recapture the environmental values that sustained island life before the arrival of Captain Cook. No one among us knows what a sustainable economy would look like as it shifted from a growth economy. On the other hand, signs of a pervasive environmental ethic have begun to appear. In recent meetings on tourism and the environment, the dialogue has at least referred to the limits of growth. Recycling, energy conservation, and litter cleanup have become consensus values for everyone from children to business leaders. Judgments from recent environmental lawsuits show us that non-profit environmental groups will now hold our county, state and federal agencies more accountable for their environmental actions. Business has begun to see that consumers prefer environmentally conscious products, packaging, and promotions. In these gathering signs of change, we have reason to hope that on these distant, small islands, we may gradually build our environmental needs into values which we can all embrace.

All of the measures that I have suggested have as an underlying purpose rethinking the belief in growth that we have unconsciously made our collective priority. They also push each of us to give *community* in its broadest sense much the same weight that we give our own wants. If these changes seem too expensive, consider how the floodtide of environmental losses already pushes us toward becoming simply another crowded place, our unique creatures and plants gone, Hawai'i all but indistinguishable from any of a dozen other sunny places. We cannot afford that, particularly if we want our children and their children to have Hawaiian islands worth inheriting, to have in their lives the exquisite cadences and beauty of the life of the land.

Right: Accessible by boat only, Nu'alolo 'Aina on the Na Pali Coast of Kaua'i has many lo'i kalo terrace sites.

Afterword

© David Boynton

There we sat on the gnarled trunk of an old Koai'e tree, perched on a bouldery slope a thousand feet above the headwaters of the Waimea River. The ancient cliffs of Waimea Canyon blushed orange in the crisp morning air as sunlight folded back the shadows of dawn.

The koai'e tree beneath us told us the story of its life. Youthful decades were spent in native dryland forest that once covered these slopes. Now amidst a tangle of lantana, just tattered forest remnants linger — halalpepe, iliau and iliahi, koa and koki'o ke'oke'o, and the venerable ohi'a lehua. Centuries of purposefully set fires have taken their toll, fires that burned the mountain slopes to leave an even growth of pili grass in their wake. Grazing cattle, hungry goats, and alien insects took up where the fires left off, until a long-forgotten storm toppled the old koai'e, leaving its twisted trunk dying on the ground.

But the koai'e persisted, as a sapling that sprouted from the old trunk just above its soil-grasping roots. The new growth prospered in slow motion until a full-grown tree now stood out firmly from the steep slope. On the branches of the fallen koai'e, yellow lichens cling, lending it a special beauty even in death.

Here is a natural symbol of the past, present, and future — a vestige of disappearing native forests, a hardy survivor of environmental degradation, and a challenge for those who cherish Hawai'i's threatened environment.

The challenge is clear, to learn as much as we can about uniquely Hawaiian species so they may survive and prosper for generations to come. Although in 1991 the koai'e was reclassified in one authoritative publication as an "undefined variety" of koa, scientists are again studying the tree in the hope of resurrecting it as a separate species worthy of protection.

The Conservation Council for Hawai'i (CCH), the islands' affiliate of the National Wildlife Federation, takes an active role in environmental protection and education. By producing posters and information about Hawaiian ecosystems for the annual Wildlife Week celebration, and through persistent legislative and regulatory activism, CCH seeks to broaden awareness of the fascination, the beauty, and the plight of Hawaiian ecosystems.

Publication of *In the Wake of Dreams* will help to refocus attention on important environmental issues. Our participation in the review process and our endorsement of this book demonstrate CCH's role in fostering awareness of the natural environment. From awareness come curiosity and concern, which in turn evolve into citizen action. *In the Wake of Dreams* is that call to action, a call that Hawai'i's citizens must heed if we are to continue to enjoy the beauty and the quality of life that these islands have provided.

If you would like to contribute to the future of the environment in Hawai'i or elsewhere, you may want to join one or more of the following environmental groups. All actively work to conserve the community of life forms in the Hawaiian Islands, and many work nationally or internationally to protect the environment.

Who to Contact

© David Boynton

Conservation Council for Hawai'i
P.O. Box 2923, Honolulu, HI 96802
Fax (808) 531-3050
Hawai'i affiliate of the
National Wildlife Federation
1400 16th St. N.W., Washington, D.C. 20036
(202) 797-6800

Earthtrust
Aikahi Park Center, Kailua HI 96734
(808) 254-2866 FAX (808) 254-6409

Environment Hawai'i Newsletter
737 Bishop St. #170-51, Honolulu, HI 96734
(808) 254-2866 FAX (808) 254-6409

Hawai'i Audubon Society
212 Merchant St. #320, Honolulu, HI 96813
(808) 528-1432
National Audubon Society
P.O. Box 52529, Boulder, CO 80322

Hawai'i Nature Center
2131 Makiki Heights Dr., Honolulu, HI 96822
(808) 955-0100

Life of the Land
19 Niolopa Pl., Honolulu, HI 96817
(808) 595-3903

Native Hawaiian Plant Society
P.O. Box 5021, Kahului, HI 96732

Natural Resources Defense Council
212 Merchant Street, #203, Honolulu, HI 96813
(808) 533-1075 FAX (808) 521-6841
National Office
1350 New York Ave. N.W.
Washington, D.C. 20005
(202) 783-7800 FAX (202) 783-5917

The Nature Conservancy of Hawai'i
1116 Smith Street, Honolulu, HI 96813
(808) 537-4508 FAX (808) 545-2019
International Headquarters
1825 North Lynn St., Arlington, VA 22209

Outdoor Circle
1110 University Ave., Honolulu, HI 96813
(808) 943-9658

Protect Kaho'olawe Ohana
1942 Naio St., Honolulu, HI 96817
(808) 845-1504

Recycling Association of Hawai'i
162 B North King St., Honolulu, HI 96817
(808) 599-1976

Sierra Club Legal Defense Fund
212 Merchant Street, #202, Honolulu, HI 96813
(808) 599-2436

Sierra Club, Hawai'i Chapter
P.O. Box 2577, Honolulu, HI 96803
(808) 538-6616
National Office
740 Polk St., San Francisco, CA 94109
(415) 776-2211

Zero Population Growth
1400 16th St., N.W., #320 Washington, D.C. 20036
(202) 332-2200

Opposite: The old Koai'e tree mentioned in the story on that page.
Above left: Lapalapa /'Olapa is a unique tree with fragrant leaves so supple they flutter gracefully, like the hula dancers that share its name.

Acknowledgements

by Paul Berry

124

© Franco Salmoiraghi

Above: One of the best Hala (Pandanus) forests near Wai'anapanapa State Park, Hana, Maui.

I find myself grateful for the talented people and reliable sources that I have been able to draw upon.

The many photographers whose images appear here deserve major credit; the beauty of their work embodies the message of nature. Their images are drawn from Tami Dawson's superb collection of nature photography, and I am grateful to Tami for her creative contribution to this book.

For their essential editorial suggestions, proofreading and other tangible support, Nancy Lawrence and Nina Berry have my heartfelt thanks.

Other valuable sources include: Patricia Tummons and her fine newsletter *Environment Hawai'i;* Peter Thompson, U.S. National Park Service Ranger on Moloka'i; Herb Kane, his art, his vision, and his fine book *Voyagers;* Sam Ka'ai, whose speech to the International Conference on Thinking several years ago became food for thought, and is excerpted here in *Postage Stamps;* David Boynton and Steven Montgomery, devoted naturalists who lent their experience and guidance; Conservation Council for Hawai'i (Hawai'i affiliate of the National Wildlife Federation) for many issues of the *Hawai'i Conserver,* S.H. Sohmer and R. Gustafson's *Plants and Flowers of Hawai'i;* Susan Scott's *Plants and Animals of Hawai'i;* The Hawai'i Audubon Society's *'Elepaio;* The Sierra Club Legal Defense Fund's *In Brief;* various publications of The Nature Conservancy of Hawai'i, including their newsletter, *Hawai'i's Extinction Crisis, Nature Conservancy Magazine,* and *The Alien Pest Species Invasion of Hawai'i* (the latter published collaboratively with the Natural

Resources Defense Council); State of Hawai'i, Department of Land and Natural Resources publications, including *Threatened and Endangered Species Plan for Wildlife, Plants, and Invertebrates*; & *Preserving Hawai'i's Natural Treasures*; The National Parks and Conservation Association *ParkWatcher*; the elegant New York Academy of Sciences publication *The Sciences*; *Smithsonian* magazine; Worldwatch Society's *Worldwatch Paper #89: National Security: The Economic and Environmental Dimensions*; and many issues of *The Wall Street Journal*; *The New York Times*; *The Honolulu Star-Bulletin*, and *The Honolulu Advertiser*.

My friend Bob Goodman has been an innovator in publishing for over a generation. After working with him as an editor on various projects over a dozen years, I can only conclude that he is three parts artist, two parts whirling dervish, and one part magician. He brings to each of his books a loving sense of the story well told, and a need to test the possibilities of new technologies in this most ancient of man's traditions. Here readers have the opportunity to see Goodman's creativity as he takes on the multiple roles of photographer, editor, designer and color desktop publisher. It is Bob's interest that has brought *In The Wake of Dreams* into being, and I am grateful for the imagination and care he has given to this message about paradise at risk.

A Publisher's Thank You...

We would like to thank Ron Seitz, the men and women of Connecting Point in Honolulu, and especially Mike Klein, who were there with answers and equipment when we were most in need.

For his friendship and for the hundreds of dedicated hours given to this project we would like to salute David Steffen, a gifted designer and computer artist whose many FreeHand illustrations grace our 32 page WhaleSong Guide to High Speed Prepress Color, and whose good taste in type and design contributed so much to In The Wake of Dreams. Thank you.

For Gwen Wock a warm Mahalo for her friendship, skill, and dedicated efforts on all of our projects including this book.

Our thanks to, Mike Falcon, Armando Herrera, Kelly Fukuhara, Michael Khoury, Joe Langdon, Ken Peer, and Lou Prestia who worked so selflessly with us to create the hundreds of scans and separations just before the arrival of Hurricane Iniki. And a special thanks to Gary Wood who came to give us a post-hurricane boost with his calm manner and great prepress skills.

To Joe Schuld and Mollie Yunker who joined us in Honolulu for what was supposed to be the last rush to the finish line. Instead, they found more ways to make the book better than we could count. We were shown new levels of organization and production efficiency. Their individual talents gave this book an entirely new dimension of quality. For that and for their friendship, we are grateful.

To so many people at Radius and Apple, Adobe, MicroNet and Aldus, and especially at Agfa—all of whom extended a helping hand over and over again as we struggled to master the new tools of high end color publishing—thank you.

For a friendship that knows few boundaries, my personal thanks to Paul Berry, who once again rode to my rescue to author this book, and support our efforts to bring it to life.

Should you ever be blessed with a Celtic friend, may he or she be modeled after the heart and talent of MacKinnon Simpson. Thank you, Mac, for everything.

To Mary Woolen, whose friendship and help when we needed it the most were always there.

A special thank you to David Boynton and Steve Montgomery for their selfless help with the captions, particularly Steve, who spent many long nights with us endlessly researching source books for the most accurate and best worded caption.

Tami Dawson's willingness to throw all her photographic resources behind our dream for this remarkable book literally made it possible. Her gifted photographer husband, Marc Schechter, took many of the photos seen throughout the book. Our appreciation as well to all the photographers she represents. They are an extraordinary group of artists.

Bob and Lorie Goodman

The Book & the Author

© Robert B. Goodman

Picture yourself with a group of friends far at sea on a beautiful Hawaiian island, a place where people live their dreams. How will you and the others know when your dreams have led you to take too much from the paradise you share? If you discover that you have gone too far, how will you stop the decline and restore what you have damaged? What is it within any of us that allows us to put so much beauty and life at risk? Can we expect man, the exploiter of nature, also to arrive as its rescuer? The answers to questions like these do not come easily, but Paul Berry's reflections on them combine with a stunning photos of island life to make for a book you'll want to have.

Now picture Hawai'i adrift in the Pacific, the microcosm of earth adrift in space. If we cannot save paradise, should we expect to save other environments? Throughout this inviting blend of anecdotes, essays, and phenomenal nature photos, Paul Berry shows us the mirror Hawai'i presents of rising environmental damage to the globe. Moving from one perspective to another, he examines the willingness and imagination we must marshall to restore paradise before we lose it. Finally he illustrates a number of ways we can use imagination, common sense, hope, and political willpower to help us recapture what is at risk. *In the Wake of Dreams* is a graceful book, one with fresh perspectives on the place of humankind in the environment, and pictures that will put nature back in the center of your heart.

Paul "Doc" Berry lives and writes in Honolulu. He teaches economics and an environmental course at a private high school.

The Agency

Photo Resource Hawai'i has been providing photography to businesses in Hawai'i and on the Mainland for the past ten years, and is Hawai'i's only stock photo agency with an extensive image collection of environmental images. Since 1990, Photo Resource has been represented worldwide by Tony Stone Images. With over 30 photographers' work on hand, (50,000 images) the Photo Resource files reflect a commitment to educate, and thereby preserve Hawai'i's unique heritage and environment. Included are images that are ideal for both advertising and editorial purposes—images that present modern Hawai'i in all its business and cultural diversity.

All of the photographs in this book are available in both low and/or high resolution digital form, or as film originals. Please contact Photo Resource Hawai'i with your needs.

You may contact any of the photographers through Photo Resource Hawai'i at 1146 Fort Street, Suite 207, Honolulu, HI, 96813, (808) 599-7773 or fax to (808) 599-7754.

The Photographers

Dave Bjorn, a photographer based on Oahu's North Shore, specializes in images which capture the unique lifestyle of that part of the island, including windsurfing and board surfing. His eye for light and color, combined with a keen imagination, create a surrealistic feeling in his images.

David Boynton, born and raised on the island of Oahu, received his B.A. in Anthropology in 1967, and a Secondary Teaching credential in 1968 in Biological Sciences from U.C.S.B. Working as a teacher, a writer, and a photographer, he has lived on Kaua'i for the past 19 years. He helped to organize the Kaua'i Group of the Sierra Club, has been an active member of the Conservation Council for Hawai'i (the local NWF affiliate), and works with the Koke'e Natural History museum. In 1990 he became the environmental resource teacher for Kaua'i District. His current project is to establish an outdoor education center in Koke'e State Park for the DOE. His broad knowledge of Hawai'i an natural history, especially birds and native flora, led to his being featured in a film on the Alaka'i Swamp, and to assisting with the filming of the Emmy award-winning National Geographic Special called "Hawai'i: Strangers in Paradise."

David prepared many of the photos captions for this book.

John S. Callahan has lived in Hawai'i for more than 20 years. A professional photographer since his graduation from U.C.L.A. in 1987, he specializes in images of the oceans of Hawai'i and the world. His assignments have taken him around the globe, and his work has appeared in more than 100 magazines and newspapers worldwide.

Monte Costa, born and raised in Hawai'i, holds a B.A. in Environmental Conservation and Management and is currently a freelance photojournalist. As staff photographer for Sea Life Park and Waimea Falls Park, her images have also been published in numerous magazines and featured in books, such as *Discovery*, *Life* and *National Geographic*. Her photos have been used by the Bishop Museum, the Polynesian Voyaging Society, the Hawai'i Maritime Center, and many others.

Tami Dawson is a photographer and the director of Photo Resource Hawai'i. She enjoys taking pictures of people in natural light, and is very grateful to have lived in Hawai'i for the past 17 years. Being an environmental enthusiast, she was very pleased to contribute her editing skills to this project.

Pat Duefrene is a graphic and exhibit designer, photographer, and writer from Kailua-Kona, on the Big Island. She has been a resident of Hawai'i for over 20 years, and has spent a great deal of time hiking, sailing, and scuba diving around the islands.

Much of her work focuses on the natural and cultural history of the Hawaiian islands. Her work has included magazine articles, historic maps and exhibits, including the Hawai'i Maritime Center where she worked as senior designer.

David Franzen has been photographing in Hawai'i for the past 15 years. His work ranges from corporate advertising to editorial and architectural interiors. His photographs have been published internationally.

Tom Gillen, president of Eagle Visions, Inc., is a photographer and Emmy award winning producer. He recently completed a series of twenty 30 second Public Service Announcements on the negative effects of alien species in Hawai'i. He is always on the lookout for grants to produce videos which express his love of the land and concern for our fragile environment.

Robert B. Goodman, a resident of Honolulu for the past 34 years, began his career as a National Geographic staff photographer when he captured the eruption of Kilauea Iki volcano on the Big Island. He photographed and co-published *The Australians* in 1967 and *The Hawai'ians* in 1971. Currently he is exploring Macintosh prepress production for his fine art books, which also generate donations for environmental protection.

Alan Goya was born and raised on Oahu. His artistic endeavors led him to San Diego, where he now resides with his wife Lynn and children, Chloe and Alexander. He once claimed the ability to turn a duffle bag into a camera.

Jack Jeffrey, a resident of Hawai'i for 18 years, is a wildlife biologist doing research on native bird and forest ecology on the Big Island. His love of birds and of photography has led him to seek out the many beautiful and unexplored places in the islands.

Val Kim was born and raised on Oahu. She now lives in Hollywood where she is a writer. In 1988 she wrote, directed and co-produced "Waging Peace", a documentary about children from Russia and the United States making peace through exchange camps during the summit talks of 1987. She continues to shoot still photography and often works in Hawai'i on movies and television commercials in various capacities.

Nikolas Konstantinou specializes in underwater photography and film production. He grew up diving with his mother, noted marine scientist Dr. Eugenie Clark. Last year Niki worked with the National Geographic Society, the Cousteau Society, the Discovery Channel, and CBS News special events. His photographs have been published locally and internationally, with a regular column in Kaua'i Magazine entitled *Treasures of the Sea*.

G. Brad Lewis, a ten year resident of the Big Island, also works out of his homes in Utah and Alaska. Specializing in environmental photography, his images of volcanoes and rainforests have appeared in Time, Life, Newsweek, Forbes, Stern, Omni, Sierra, Outside, and many others. His fine art prints are shown internationally.

Steven Lee Montgomery has worked intensively, beginning in 1968, for legislation which created a state network of reserves to protect samples of Hawai'i's native plant and animal communities, and geological sites. He worked for six years as the State Natural Areas Specialist. At the University of Hawai'i, he earned a Ph.D. degree in entomology. Because of Steve's discovery of new trees, herbs, and insects, a dozen island species were named after him.

He was both a subject of, and a scientific advisor for, the Emmy award-winning National Geographic Special called "Hawai'i: Strangers in Paradise." Currently, in addition to biological consulting, he is a Research Associate at Bishop Museum. He is the president of the Oahu Chapter of the Conservation Council for Hawai'i, and represents the Council at the National Wildlife Federation conferences.

Steve assisted with the natural history facts for the photo captions.

William P. Mull is a research assistant in entomology with the Bishop Museum. He lives in Volcano Village on the Big Island and has been studying Hawai'i biota for 25 years. He is the foremost photographer of native Hawaiian land invertebrates and is the co-author of the new book, *Hawai'i's Insects and their Kin*, published by University of Hawai'i Press, 1992.

Kenneth M. Nagata works at the U.S. Dept. of Agriculture in the plant protection and quarantine division. A botanical consultant, he is the author of *Hawai'i's Vanishing Flora*. He is also affiliated with the Bishop Museum's botany department.

Jon K. Ogata, a Honolulu based photographer, was born and raised on the island of Kaua'i. His work includes travel, environmental, nature, and scenic subject matter. He shoots with both 35 mm and medium format cameras. Jon is a long-time member of the Sierra Club.

Franco Salmoiraghi has lived and photographed in Hawai'i since 1968. His photographs are featured in many books and periodicals locally and internationally.

Franco's work reflects an intent to photograph the landscape, its people and places, clearly and directly so that the true essence of their spirit is illuminated.

His black and white photographic prints of Hawai'i are treasured and extensively represented in the collection of the Hawai'i State Foundation on Culture and the Arts and many other public and private collections.

Marc Schechter has specialized in advertising and editorial photography for over 15 years. A resident of Hawai'i for over 25 years, his studio is located in the heart of downtown Honolulu. His talents include his gentle and caring approach with people, his sense of humor, and his fine tuned sense of technical and artistic excellence.

James Wellner currently resides on Oahu, with credits in many of the magazines published in Hawai'i, as well as in national and foreign publications. Working commercially as an editorial/corporate/ and architectural photographer, his personal work is often surreal and vibrantly colorful.

Doc White lives in San Diego and has been sailing most of his life. For over 15 years he has devoted himself to diving, professional underwater photography and photographic support, scientific research, and seamanship. In 1981 he built a 45 foot dive and film vessel, *Mirage*, from which he continued his professional activity, gaining commendations for his photography, technologically advanced equipment, and superb seamanship from notable figures connected with marine endeavors in every part of the world.

Publisher's Production Notes

In the words of Yogi Berra, "It was *deja vu* all over again." Amazingly, we went through all the steps of creating this book twice!

The first time was pure hubris. In order to see just how productive this new technology could be, we set out to create an all color coffeetable book on the Macintosh desktop in the fastest possible time—a World Land Speed Record! Could we achieve real throughput and still produce superb color quality?

To answer that question, we brought in the finest desktop technology we could gather, invited a few of our closest associates to join us for the adventure, and fired the starting pistol. From that moment on, days seemed to flow one into the other, and our lives ceased to be our own. As we flew through the layouts, it was the best of times and the worst of times all rolled into one

We set-up Mac IIs with DayStar 50 accelerators and internal Fujitsu drives, two Quadras, each with a pair of Radius Rocket boards installed. Each Radius Rocket had a SCSI 2 booster card attached so that it could read and write to its own MicroNet 635 meg drive.

Monitors were Radius PrecisionColor 20's and 19's for the simple reason that together with their accelerated video cards, they are the best monitors we know. We also believe in pairing equipment from the same manufacturer wherever possible., e.g. Rocket boards with Radius monitors etc.

For storage devices we ordered a fleet of MicroNet drives; Ravens for the Quadras, SCSI II drives as standalones; both large and small SONY magneto-optical drives; SyQuest 44s (since replaced with the new 44/88's); plus SONY DAT drives for back-ups.

For memory we chose Newer Technology and their well engineered memory chips. In addition, we placed our entire master operating system on the Newer DART-128 drive, a bullet-proof RAM drive with a built-in uninterruptable power system. During the entire project we felt absolutely safe from the sudden power outages that afflict Honolulu.

To add to our productivity, we also installed DayStar RAM PowerCards, each with 64 megabytes of RAM. If this sounds like a "Dream" system, you're quite right. It was.

FreeHand Illustrations by David Steffen

Quadra 950
with Radius
Rocket 33's

Radius Precision
Color Display/20
and Macintosh IIfx

130

MicroNet/SONY
128 Magneto
Optical drive

MicroNet 2.6 Gigabyte
external Raven Disk Array

Newer Technology
128 megabyte Dart
Ram drive with built-in
U.P.S.

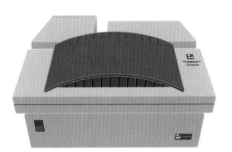

PixelCraft 4520RS
transparency scanner

Was it overkill? Hardly.

There was more. As closely as possible, we wanted to emulate a mid-sized service bureau, or a corporate in-house publishing installation. That meant putting our Macintosh computers on a network. We chose Novell 3.1.1 Netware for Macintosh which required a DOS server and a second P.C. (an Argent 486/DX33 from Computer Source in Atlanta) as an administrator. The most powerful DOS machine we knew was the Hewlett-Packard 486 Vectra 50U EISA which we filled with 20 megabytes of RAM and two powerful 32-bit ethernet cards from Eagle Technologies. A 2-gigabyte MicroNet drive completed that assembly.

Ethernet Phase 2 connected all of our computers and printers. We have been converts to Asanté Technologies ethernet products for years. Their engineering, price, and service are exemplary.

To really up the ante in transferring data between our computers, we installed the Augment Systems fiber-optic AL-101 Retriever boards. This gave us file transfers 10-15 times faster than ethernet.

Scanning was handled by a pair of BarneyScan 4520 RS transparency scanners plus an AGFA Horizon flatbed. The BarneyScan (now the Pro Imager 4520 RS from PixelCraft, A Xerox Company) together

with PixelCraft's industry leading QuickScan and Color Access software, gave us the ability to crank out a constant four scans per hour per operator per machine. That's four scans retouched, color corrected, unsharp masked, and readied for batch separation that took place every night unattended.

Our imagesetter of choice was the AGFA SelectSet 7000 together with AGFA ZHN film. The RIPS (in early Beta form) were the AGFA MultiStar 400 and Star 600 units that more than doubled the output from our 7000. Our throughput was truly exceptional.

Both RIPS had halftone accelerators installed, and since everything about the RIPS was new and untested in the real world, we had the fun and frustration of helping AGFA turn out a pair of real thoroughbreds.

Film was processed in a compact and self-plumbed AGFA Rapiline 28 processor that is the most trouble-free piece of equipment I've ever experienced.

Densities and calibration were handled by three densitometers from X-Rite, our original baby portable X-Rite 341, and its bigger X-Rite 361 for film and X-Rite 416 for reflective measurements.

All during the page assembly process we made endless checkproofs on our 600 dpi QMS 815 printers. Contract proofing was on Agfaproof using the small PRS 2 unit. Our printing frame, as always, was the OVAC 24 from OLEC Corporation, now with a newly available blanket that speeds drawdown time with Agfaproof.

Registration of film and proofs was achieved using the SelectSet 7000 built-in registration punch together with the Stoesser Pin Register System.

Our software was the entire suite of Aldus products—from PageMaker to FreeHand to TrapWise and PressWise.

Adobe Photoshop, as it has been from the beginnings of the WhaleSong Project, was at the center of every scan. Our type was from The Font Company in Scottsdale, AZ.

The goal was to do all the prepress for a 160 page book in six days, and on the seventh have a big party. That meant scanning in all the color, correcting and retouching it, creating the color separations, placing the images into a predesigned layout, flowing in preset type, proofing everything, creating final film on the imagesetter, and shipping it all off to the printer. Miraculously, we did all the color in 174 hours. But fate intervened to keep the book from the printer.

Hurricane Iniki swept in and threw all our elaborate plans into the proverbial cocked hat. Our studio escaped with only minor damage, but the power was out for more than a day, and it took us three days to put everything back in place, strip the boards from windows, and feel normal. We missed our printer's slot and our bindery slot.

The delay yielded tangible benefits. We had time to show the layouts to conservationists who made many suggestions that improved the text and our picture selection. Because our new equipment made changes so easy, the book you hold in your hand is not the book that emerged at the 174 hour mark, but a better and lovelier descendant of that book.

Besides humility, our attempt at a prepress world land speed record taught us:

First, that real productivity and quality are achievable on the Macintosh desktop today.

Second, that we chose the right equipment; we recommend it without reservation.

Third, that when you absolutely must get the work out, speed and power are essential.

Fourth, that throughout all the repetitive prepress tasks, speed generates additional time for creativity—time to massage text and pictures and still meet deadlines. We hope you enjoy *In The Wake of Dreams.*

Bob Goodman

To order additional copies of this book, or of the 32 page *WhaleSong Guide to High Speed Prepress Color,* please call Toll Free 1-800-922-5599.

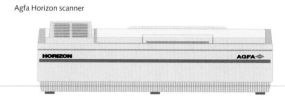

Agfa Horizon scanner

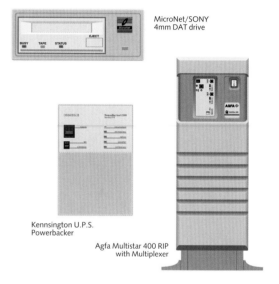

MicroNet/SONY 4mm DAT drive

Kennsington U.P.S. Powerbacker

Agfa Multistar 400 RIP with Multiplexer

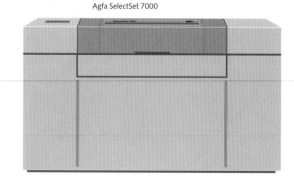

Agfa SelectSet 7000